CW01082751

BEDTIME STORIES FOR KIDS

A Fantastic Collection of Short Stories for Children and Toddlers to Help Them Relax, Fall Asleep Quickly and Learn Mindfulness and Meditation to Be Inspired and Thrive

By Andy Potter & Sonia Ferrigno

Table of contents

Introduction

This collection of short stories for children has been created in the attempt of providing your child with the ideal sleep mode. It includes some enchanting bedtime stories, which children will definitely want to read before falling into their own dreamlands.

These stories aim to teach some fundamental ideals, in an inferred and endearing way, with which children can equate. Each narrative will help children relax and open up their creative minds to connect with enchanting and imaginary worlds. This stimulation of the creativity, along with the underlying adventures the stories reveal, is excellent for the development of the child's mind and intelligence.

Now close your eyes, listen and smell. Imagine you're someone else, and somewhere you've never been before in quest of adventure, in search of the truth. Dream, always dream, because when you dream you can do anything you want, go wherever you wish. And who knows, maybe one day one of your dreams may come true.

This collection of short stories tells the tales of children like you who have dreams, hopes and desires. In these stories, magical things happen, and dreams come true, or they unveil truths that they had never suspected before. Their adventures will lead you to foreign lands, to enchanting woods and balmy oceans. You will hear about the power of nature and love, while you lay your cheek on your pillow and snuggle up under the duvet. But best of all, you will go with them on their adventures and discover how simple events can turn out to be quite extraordinary.

This collection of short stories humorously and magically explores such things that are sometimes invisible to the human eye. Each tale allows us to peek into the lives of children who live seemingly ordinary lives, just like you. Sometimes, however, they find themselves involved in wondrous and magical situations. At times the heroes of the adventures are not human at all but are nonetheless charming and adorable.

From the Hawaiian Islands to the Land of the Rising Sun, the characters of these stories will take you along with them on their enchanting exploits. You may venture into bewitched woods at night or step into a sweet shop unlike any you've seen before. Or again, you might find yourself up in a hot air balloon with a couple of singular characters in a race towards the impossible.

Whomever you follow in their adventure, you'll be captivated by their story and be lulled by their charm until you fall asleep. And who knows, you too may find yourself living one of their adventures in your dreams.

An Unusual Summer's Eve Dinner

When the crickets start their relentless high-pitched chirping and the days stretch out until the late evening hours, we finally heave a sigh of relief. Summer is here at last.

Those endless hours spent in the classroom are almost behind us and the smell of freedom whiffs through the open windows, drifting along with the warm summer breeze.

My family and I have a special summer event at the beginning of every summer. No matter what happens we always and without fail open the summer season with a family dinner at our favourite restaurant overlooking the lake.

This year was no exception. I was at once fretting with anticipation and apprehensive in case a sudden summer thunderstorm should spoil our treat and disrupt our family ritual.

Although it was merely the end of June, the heat was already sweltering hot. While I admit that rain and more refreshing winds are sometimes welcome, they certainly are not for our special event.

I've noticed that summer thunderstorms seem to have an annoying quirk. They turn up when least expected and most times are indeed unwelcome.

Storms are generally very temperamental in our region, and before you know it, they strike and ruin your plans. Which was why I was jittery for the next week and my sister Jenny was not happy at all, choosing to ignore me thinking that I wouldn't survive. Little does my younger sister suspect that I am more than happy to adapt to her whim.

The last Saturday evening before the end of term finally arrived, so did a clear cobalt-blue sky and warm summer breeze.

As we drove down the potholed country road towards the lake, I noticed that the pastures were already turning yellow burnt by the sun's harshness and sparse rainfall. The lake, however, glowed intensely turquoise and seemed alive with glitter as the ripples on the water's surface caught the lazy evening sun rays.

My father parked on the grass bank along the road at the edge of the restaurant's garden. The premises don't boast a large parking lot, so if you were expecting an exclusive dining setting, you were wrong. Our restaurant is an open-air family-run affair attached to a small and friendly camping ground, bustling with activity and chatter.

A tall and enormous bellied man came to greet us with a broad grin and beaming eyes. Yes, you guessed, he's the owner and can be excruciatingly tiresome when he starts talking. Fortunately, he didn't have time to dawdle in small talk. All the tables were taken except ours, nestled in the far corner of the terrace overlooking the majestic lake.

"Oh my favourite family," he declared, opening his arms and hugging my father with fervour. Then he took my mother's hand and kissed it gallantly. I slipped a side glance at my sister, and we both pulled faces. She tried to suppress a giggle as she sought refuge behind me anticipating the worst.

Sure enough, our host patted me on the head with enthusiasm, a bit too vigorously to my taste.

"Ah, my little king is back for the summer opening feast," he chuckled with a wink and then knelt down behind me to smack a giant kiss on Jenny's forehead. He then went on to marvel at how much we had grown since last year.

Again I thought how ridiculously absurd adults can be. What did he expect? Of course, we'd grown! It was also dreadfully embarrassing to be called 'king'. A title he had honoured me with a few years ago and had decided I should adopt as a nickname from then on.

All had started when I was just out of my baby stage at one of our dinners. Apparently, once I had been foolish enough to retort that I was nobody's "little boy" to our host, who in turn, amused at my indignation had replied, "Oh really? What shall I call you then?"

Instead of stating the obvious, I had regrettably announced that he could call me 'my king'. This of course, had triggered off a wave of roaring laughter among the adults, and unfortunately, the nickname stuck.

Today, he took us to our table without further preamble, as there was quite a crowd to feed that evening. I sat down with anticipation, already relishing the delicious pizza I was going to devour.

Sandra, one of the waitresses whom I suspect, is a family member, came to us with a beam and kissed both

Jenny and me in a more subdued manner. I like Sandra, I could take a kiss from her any day without complaining.

Our parents ordered our drinks. A special dinner treat and a welcome change from the water we have to drink at the table every day. You would expect at least a soft drink at weekends once in a while, I mean that's not asking much is it? But no, only on our rare outings are we allowed a delicious boost of sheer sugary pleasure.

I had a feeling the wait would be a long one this evening, so I took leave from the table with the excuse of a wizz, that's what we call a pressing need at home. Then I followed the path up from behind the restaurant that led to the toilets and camping grounds.

I could smell sausages cooking somewhere in the campsite, and the delicious fragrance filled my nostrils and set my stomach groaning fiercely. I scanned the tents and thought I could just about catch a glimpse of bluish smoke rising lazily behind a small green tent to the left, under the shelter of a beech tree.

I turned around to go back towards the toilets when I felt a sudden swirl around my bare ankles. My first thought was that a cat had wrapped its bushy tail around them, expecting to find the furry culprit when I looked down. To my utter amazement, there was no cat. What I did see was an eerie whirl of blue smoke eddying around my legs, and tickling them gently. The next thing I knew the turmoil of bluish smoke started pulling at me.

The evening light darkened dramatically all of a sudden, and when I looked up I gasped in horror. Dark and looming clouds had thickened tightly together and grew menacingly massive by the second.

Around me, loose leaves and odd bits of sticks started to whip around and dance frantically in the muggy wind charged with humidity and electricity. The bluish smoke that had merely danced lightly around my ankles and calves now whooshed, pulling and tugging at me.

I felt a large, heavy drop plop on my cheek. Then another one hit my bare leg, followed by another and another. Soon the large drops of rain teamed up in a mass of water and the rain came pounding down.

The bluish smoke persisted relentlessly, now yanking me along into the perimeter of the camping grounds. I felt myself being dragged towards the very tent I had noticed just a moment before. Then swish! The smoke enveloped me from head to toe frantically eddying from my head to my toes. I closed my eyes in dread.

Then, just as it had appeared, it vanished. The whooshing sound was replaced by the violent rat-a-tat of the giant raindrops on the scorched grass.

I opened my eyes and there standing in front of the open tent was a strikingly pretty girl with eyes alive and twinkling mischievously. She was holding a stick in her hand, and at the end of the stick was a deliciously smelling sausage.

"Come on," she said impatiently, "what are you doing standing in the rain? I've been waiting for you."

"If you don't get a move on our dinner will get cold," she added with a pout, then turned around and disappeared through the opening.

If it hadn't been for the unpleasant feel of the rain, I would have stood there open-mouthed not daring to move for who knows how long. As it was, the dampness and stickiness seeping through my t-shirt dragged me out of my reverie, so I stepped in through the open tent.

Sausages? Sausages?!? There weren't just sausages in the tent. I was greeted by the most breath-taking banquet of food I had ever set eyes on.

The table set up in the centre of the little green tent was the size of a wedding reception. Strewn all along the large table were delicacies of all sorts. The smell of tasty barbecued meats filled the tent, and the view was irresistibly alluring.

The girl was seated on an odd-looking chair. It actually looked like a throne of some sort. Then I noticed another very unusual object propped on top of her head.

A crown! I couldn't believe my eyes. She was wearing a crown!

She gestured towards another chair at the opposite end of the table and announced with dignity, "sit down my king. The feast is about to begin!" She then clapped her hands twice, and two maids dressed in long robes appeared through the opening of the tent and stood in front of the table patiently.

The girl with the crown clapped her hands for a second time, and two young men walked in, they too were clad in odd costumes. One carried what looked like an odd-shaped guitar and the other a flute. They stood behind her throne and as if on cue started to play a mellow ballad.

One of the maids took my hand and led me to the end of the table where another throne-like chair was waiting. I was obviously expected to sit down and did so gratefully as I feared my legs would soon buckle under me.

Hands clapped again, and the maids went to work. One by one they presented my host and me with platters of meats, fish, and delicate pastries.

What could I do? I couldn't refuse. Besides, the rain outside was strumming relentlessly on the tent, and the wind was lashing powerfully, making the opening to flap fiercely against the tent.

So I dutifully ate and savoured the delicious food my mysterious dining partner had provided me with, without a second thought for my family. I was mesmerized by the atmosphere the scrumptious smells rising from the royal banquet spread before me, but what really transfixed me was sitting opposite me.

The girl with the crown. The queen of the feast, who was now watching me from across the table with an amused smile as she too enjoyed the feast.

I felt like a real king on this extraordinary summer's eve. I was the king of the tent, the king of the camping site and indeed the king of the world. And opposite me was my queen, whoever she was she looked ethereal and exquisitely beautiful.

I never thought that girls could look like this before. I suddenly felt extremely vulnerable and powerful at the same time, the crown on my head imposingly reminding me of my stature.

The meal seemed to linger endlessly while the music filled the tent with tenderness and dreamlike images. Objects floated around me and my queen's eyes shined brightly in the dim light of the tent.

The rain stopped just as suddenly as it had started; the music too. The two young musicians retreated bowing reverently as they backed out of the tent and the maids followed carrying empty trays as they left.

I looked across the table. My host was no longer a queen, the crown now lay discarded on the table. The once queen was already walking towards the entrance of the tent, beckoning me to follow with her teasing smile and enchanting eyes.

I stood up regretfully and walked into the reality of the summer evening once more. My eyes had to readjust to the strangely harsh and stark evening light.

I looked up and gasped in sheer amazement. Not one cloud remained in the sky. They had all dispersed as if by magic. The blue cobalt colour was turning into a purplish hue as the daylight slipped from the sun's clutches and darkness regained its rightful place.

I had been so enthralled by the sky that I had forgotten about the mysterious girl. When I looked down, she was gone. The entrance to the tent was zipped closed, and all was still and calm once more.

Reluctantly, I made my way back to the restaurant still dizzy and in shock. I was expecting it to be empty and wondered where all the restaurant guests had taken refuge during the storm.

To my surprise, when I stepped on to the terrace, it was as crowded as before. I spotted our table in the far corner, my parents and Jenny still waiting for the pizzas.

I meandered between the tables towards them still in a daze, and as I was about to sit down, Sandra arrived with the first two pizzas.

"Here you are, Jacob and Jenny! House special for you today," she said joyfully. Then added winking at me, "a real feast for a king tonight!"

The words hit me as eerie, and I watched as she walked away, wondering if she had anything to do with the weird experience I had just walked away from.

I stared at the gigantic pizza on my plate. How could I possibly eat that now? My stomach was bursting after the feast. Or was it?

I looked around at my family as they joyfully tucked into the food, my appetite lost, and my thoughts wandering back to my queen. I had been king today for the first time, and it was a wonderful feeling.

As Invisible as the Wind

Little Tommy looked out of the classroom window. The drone of the teacher's monotonous voice hummed in the distance as he watched the leaves frolicking in the wind. Oh, how delightful it would be to dance and shake about as the autumn leaves instead of sitting in a classroom trying to keep awake. Little Tommy didn't care much for school. He preferred to be outside and sit under the big tree in the playground, reading his favourite books about animals. He wasn't one for climbing trees or running games all he wanted to do was sit outside under the shade of the trees or watch the birds as they flew from branch to branch collecting sticks and grass for their nests. Little Tommy also spent hours watching the ants climb up the tree trunk carrying enormous loads on their tiny bodies. Tommy's teacher shook his head when he got his sums wrong, or that time he couldn't spell caterpillar correctly. Still, Tommy knew everything there was to know about caterpillars, so it didn't really matter if he had forgotten the R, he was sure the caterpillar wouldn't mind.

Tommy watched again as the wind swept the leaves along the pathway leading from the school out towards the park. If only he could be invisible like the wind and fly out of the classroom window to the great oak tree near the lake. The hum of the teacher grew fainter and fainter, and Tommy's eyelids grew heavier as he followed the swirling leaves along the pathway.

Suddenly the window flew open, and Tommy's pencil case flipped on the floor with a clatter of pens and pencils. He quickly knelt to tidy the mess, expecting the teacher to yell at him for his clumsiness. But no sound came, no scolding or shout. Tom looked up gingerly, and his eyes widened in surprise. Not only was the teacher not looking at him, no one else was either. Nobody had heard the window slam or the clatter of the pens on the floor. Strange. He got up hastily and accidentally knocked the back of the chair in front of him. No reaction. Polly, who was sitting in the chair, didn't turn around to scowl at him as she usually did. It was as if she hadn't noticed him at all. Tommy cleared his throat once, then a second time but louder. Nobody turned around.

Was that possible? Had he become invisible as he had wished? Slowly, Tommy walked between the desks towards the teacher, his shoulders hunched up, expecting the teacher to bellow at him to return to his desk.

Again, no-one even blinked, and the teacher continued with his drone and looked right through him.

"I'm invisible," cried Tommy, skipping out of the classroom into the corridor, and without a second thought, Tommy clambered down the stairs and out of the front entrance. He felt like the wind as he ran up the path, dancing with the leaves while gusts of air whirled around him.

A lady with a pram was strolling near the small lake humming a tune to a sleeping baby. Tommy said a polite, "Good morning," but the lady never looked up once.

"I truly am invisible," cried Tommy at the top of his voice. He stopped in his tracks and thought. Now that I'm invisible, I can do what I want. I can go to the library and choose one of my favourite books. I'll go and sit in the park under the large oak near the lake and read all day. The park was out of bounds during school hours and so was the library unless you had special permission. So Tommy trotted happily up the path, along with the wind swirling the leaves and pushed the library door open. Mrs Marvel, the librarian, was writing something in a large book but didn't look up when Tommy swept in like the autumn breeze. He was as invisible as a draft of air and as free as the wind. He went to the animal section and chose a book on caterpillars and tucked it under his arm. Before leaving the school building again, Tommy had a second thought as his tummy started to rumble. He headed down to the cafeteria and heard the clinking of plates and cutlery as the kitchen staff prepared for lunch. He passed by the bread baskets and took two slices of bread right under the nose of the bad-tempered cook. Then he went to the tray of sliced cheese and ham and made himself an enormous sandwich right there in front of the three kitchen helpers. "I'm as invisible as the wind," shouted Tommy and ran out of the kitchen laughing and skipping. With the caterpillar book under one arm and the sandwich wrapped in a paper napkin, he ran out of the school entrance and onto the pathway. The sun was peeking out from behind the clouds, and the autumn wind picked up and spun around him in warm whiffs. The leaves swirled around Tommy's feet and joined Tommy as he skipped towards the park and the grand old oak tree. As he settled under the large canopy, Tommy nestled the large book on his knees and opened it with one hand, while with the other he held the cheese and ham sandwich and took a large bite. The pages flipped by themselves as the warm autumn flurry spun around the tree where Tommy was huddled, and Tommy read whatever page happened to please the wind. He stayed under the tree all afternoon. The children came out in the playground at lunchtime, then went back into class while Tommy sat and read his caterpillar book his eyes gleaming with joy and his ears filled with the wind's whisper. Nobody noticed the little boy under the giant old oak. He was as invisible and as free as the wind, and as happy as he had ever been. Once again, the playground filled with shouts and laughter and still Tommy's eyes hovered over the pages of his beloved book, as the wind wrapped him in its invisible veil. The birds and the rustling leaves were his only companions until the sun started to lean over to the west, and the whirl of the wind began to quieten.

As suddenly as the autumn wind had picked up, it stopped. The leaves fell lifeless to the ground, and the reassuring whisper of Tommy's invisible companion ceased. The same woman he had seen that morning went past him with the pram singing her lullaby, but this time she looked up and smiled a Tommy then continued towards the small lake.

Tommy then realised that with the wind had gone his invisible power. It was now time to go back to the playground and join the other children waiting in line for the end of day bell. As he got up a last gust of air enveloped him, and together they drifted through the park and into the playground then it wavered and vanished.

Polly came up to Tommy and scowled at him. "When did you get that book then? It's not library day today."

"I became invisible and went past Mrs Marvel and took it right from under her nose," replied Tommy looking straight into Polly's mean little eyes. Polly stuck up her nose and clicked her tongue, then turned her back on him.

Tommy grinned and then laughed and laughed, as he had never laughed before. He looked up at the sky and wondered if the wind would come the next day and take him on another invisible journey.

Bad News

Here I was, ready to introduce myself, and what happens? Our father announced during supper that we were going to change house!

When he told my sister and me that we were going to move, we both went on a hunger strike. Of course, we did, what else could we do? Except refuse to make our beds, or paint the neighbour's cat bright pink, there was no other possible solution. But the cat is another story, and my legs get shaky just mentioning the cat.

Now, a hunger strike is no simple feat for me, let alone for my sister Jenny, who is only five and still in kindergarten. I really had a hard time trying to convince her that this was all for an excellent cause. Our house was in danger.

"No breakfast? Jenny gasped," but I can't give up my honey loops, I'm hungry. No, I'm starffing," she added, her pleading big blue eyes already flooding with tears.

"You can't be starving, we've just had supper," I said, raising my eyes in exasperation. This wasn't going to be easy. I had to think up something fast. Then, I had a sudden brainwave.

I bribed my sister with my hidden stock of sweets - Mum doesn't know about those, so the hunger strike was saved.

The morning after our parents served us the gloomy news, we both marched down the stairs with determined faces and sat across from our father, who was hiding behind his newspaper.

Does he really think we are so gullible as to believe he's actually reading behind there? I'm sure it's an excuse to keep the breakfast noise down. Kid chit chat obviously irritates grown-ups. I wonder if they realise the hypocrisy of it all. They go on and on, while we can hardly open our mouths.

In fact, I know he isn't reading the news at all. I have photographs to prove it. Yes, *real* photographs.

I took some snaps of him while he was pretending to read. He thought I was taking pictures of the garden behind him. No one pays attention when I take photos, they are used to me going about with my camera around my neck. It's a cool Polaroid camera my uncle gave me last Christmas. A snap, and out comes the real thing.

When I want to figure something out, I take lots of photos, then I stick them up on the wall in a row, and study them carefully. Most of the time, the solution comes quickly. If not, I need to take some more just to make sure.

After having studied numerous snapshots of our father, I am now sure he uses his reading sessions to impress us. If he thinks we can be duped, he can think twice. He can also think twice about changing houses. I was never going to leave my best friend - well, my only one -, my favourite hiding places and, most of all, my cherished sweet shop at the end of our street.

So there we were, Jenny and I, trying to look as stoic and determined as we could, waiting patiently for our father to lower his newspaper. I caught Jenny's eyes lingering too long on the cereal box and tugged at her sleeve. She sighed, heaved her elbows up on the dining table, then rested her pointed chin in her hands.

Not hearing the usual crunching noises - further proof that our dad could not have been reading if he had noticed the silence - he lowered the newspaper. His eyebrows rose when he saw that we were both just sitting there staring at him.

"Oh," he chided, "are you about to own up to some mischief?"

I cleared my throat, straightened my shoulders and announced, "we are on a hunger strike to protest against a decision we do not agree with."

"Hear! Hear!" Jenny added, waking from her lethargy.

Our father looked puzzled. Had he no idea of the disruption he was causing? I felt even more affronted.

"You are what?" he asked incredulously.

"We are on a hunger strike," echoed Jenny raising her chin with dignity.

Just then, our mother came in through the door that leads from the dining room into the kitchen. She was holding a pot of steaming tea, which she held at an awkward angle while she managed to pop two slices of bread in the toaster. I'm not fond of tea, but I must admit that morning I would have gulped down anything.

"Well dear, I think we have a crisis this morning," said our father nodding towards us, and finally putting his paper down. "It seems your children are on strike."

Why was it that we were always Mum's kids when we didn't behave as our dad wanted us to?

"They are?" replied our mum sitting down opposite Jenny and me, and pouring herself a cup of tea. She didn't seem in the least worried or anxious about us starving to death. We had already been deprived of the most important meal of the day, and here they were going on as if nothing was happening.

And what was more, our dad hid behind the newspaper again.

I was about to say something crucial when Jenny's stomach grumbled loudly. She clutched at it and tried to suppress a giggle.

That's when it all happened. Just like that. I'm not sure if it was Jenny's groaning stomach or my fiery indignation at our parents' insensibility, but the newspaper went up in flames.

As if on cue, the teapot started shaking madly, and steam came shooting out of its spout. Hot tea bubbled out and spilt onto the table. Next, the chocolate cereal balls shot out from the box in all directions, and Jenny jumped up on the chair trying to catch them with her open mouth.

My head began spinning madly as I watched the chocolate balls swirling above Jenny's head. She was snatching at them in glee and stuffing them into her mouth.

Across the table, Dad was still holding on to the burning newspaper as if nothing was wrong, further proof that he was not reading it. Mum was staring at the teapot as if that was how teapots usually behaved at breakfast time.

The next thing I knew the toast popped out of the toaster. It shot up so high in the air that I had time to catch both pieces before they fell to the floor. To top it all, the knife jumped up and danced across the butter, then slapped the two pieces of toast with the deliciously looking spread.

What could I do? The two pieces of toast were there in my hands, ready to be eaten. I stole a glance at our mother, who was intent on the steaming teapot and at my father surrounded by flames. Closing my eyes, I dug into the fragrant toast and ate the lot with relish, oblivious of the frenzy around me.

While I was munching on my last mouthful, Jenny's chocolate pops froze in mid-air and plopped one by one back into the box. The teapot stopped piping with a fading sizzle, and Dad's newspaper went up in smoke.

All was quiet again. Dad broke the silence with a sigh and exclaimed, "I don't know why I read the newspaper every morning, it's full of rubbish anyway. I could just as well use it to light the fire," he added, getting up and leaving the dining room with his empty cup in hand.

Mum looked over her teacup at Jenny and asked, "Was that your tummy rumbling Jenny? That must mean you're hungry, mustn't it?"

"Oh no," my sister answered firmly, I'm not at all hungry this morning, mummy."

I stared at my sister, open-mouthed. Of course, she wasn't hungry, she had just scoffed a whole pack of cereal, and I, two large pieces of toast with delicious butter.

Or had we?

Gandalf and the Missing Underwear

"No, no, no and no, drop that right now Gandalf!" I scolded tugging at one of my favourite blue and black striped socks. Our five-month-old black cocker spaniel pulled back, his silky ears flopping about wildly.

"Grrr," growled our pup playfully.

"Don't you grrr at me naughty pup," I said, frowning as menacingly as I could and chiding him with my forefinger.

He sat down and let go of the sock. His ears flopped back down around his shiny, fluffy face and fell back along his neck as he looked up gingerly at me. His large dark brown eyes searched mine through his impossibly long eyelashes. It was very hard not to pick him up and cuddle him for comfort. But he had to learn how to behave. I needed my socks as well as my underwear. I had to teach him to stop this bad habit of his; besides he had loads of toys to chew on.

"We won't have any more socks left if you keep shredding them to bits," I scolded again, nervously glancing over my shoulder towards the kitchen.

Mum had repeatedly warned my sister and me that if our dog destroyed our underwear and socks, it was our own fault.

"If your rooms were tidier he wouldn't find any socks or pants to chew on would he?" she had said, with her typically cool air that meant 'I told you so'. "If that dog eats up all your socks and underwear, then you'll just have to go without!"

Miranda had gasped out loud, her eyes wide with terror as she watched Mum turn around, head high and march out of the bedroom.

Her gaze was transfixed on the open doorway, her mouth still open, but no word came out. She finally turned, her eyes filled with anxiety and jumped on her bed. She then tucked her knees under her chin and wrapped her hands around her legs, as she usually does when she's unhappy about something.

"Oh dear Jay Jay, imagine going to school without underwear," she wailed, "what if they pull up my skirt? Some nasty boys in school think it's funny."

My sister always calls me Jay Jay when she needs comforting. Most of the time, however, she always tries to act aloof and haughty, wanting to play the role of the intellectual kid. She thinks Jacob is a very snobbish name and likes to say it often just to tease me.

I lifted my eyes to the ceiling at her ludicrous fear. Still, I realised she was obviously anxious about the possibility. So I jumped on the bed next to her.

"I really can't imagine how anyone could go to school forgetting to put their underpants on."

"Oh no, I would never forget something as important as that... at least I hope not," Miranda said, turning to look at me, her large blue eyes filled with despair. "But what if Gandalf chews them all up?"

"Miranda!" I sighed impatiently, "How do think he could possibly manage such a feat. Do you realise how many underwear and socks we have?"

I slipped off her bed, irritated with this silly talk. I had more important things to get on with, I had to finish my homework fast and get working on my model WWII warplane.

"You'll just have to do as mum says then and tidy your stuff."

I walked out of the room, glancing back briefly at the doorway. Miranda's face was a mask of desperation,

I nearly felt sorry for her, but I was busy now. I would check back on her later.

When I decided to check on her again half an hour later, the door was closed, and I could hear her bustling about noisily. Ha, ha, I thought, she's tidying up then finally. So, I just walked past her room and into the garden to the workshop where my piece of art was waiting.

The next morning when I looked out of the window there was frost on the ground. Winter was definitely round the corner. I swung my bare feet on the floor and shivered, the wooden floor felt cold, and the thought of the freezing morning sent a shiver through me.

I picked up a pair of jeans and a sweatshirt from the floor and swooped up the rest of the scattered clothes at the base of the bed and stuffed them under my duvet before Mum noticed the mess. I opened the top drawer where I was supposed to keep my socks and underwear and took a pair of socks out. I must admit it was in a bit of a jumble and I had to rummage about for the underwear. I frowned as I turned over a few lone socks, a cricket ball and a pair of swimming trunks. No underwear. At that point, I panicked and rushed to the bathroom to check the laundry basket. Empty. I zoomed back to the bedroom and looked under the bed, on the bookshelf and in the other drawers of the wardrobe. No pants.

That's when I knew I was in trouble. Our pup had taken all the underwear and Mum would have a fit! I had to find them and fast before Mum found out. I lifted the duvet and sighed with relief. In the pile of clothes I had picked up from the floor, there was one clean pair. At least I had underwear for today. Then a thought struck me, and I rushed to Miranda's bedroom, but she had already gone down to breakfast. I pulled open her drawer, and sure enough, no underwear either, only socks!

When I went down to breakfast, I noticed Miranda still had her pyjamas on as it was a Saturday and we weren't going to school. Luckily she hadn't noticed that her underwear had disappeared too. I had to find out where

Gandalf had buried it hoping he hadn't chewed all of it up.

That morning while Miranda and Mum were in the kitchen baking a cake, I let Gandalf out in the garden. I hid in the shed spying on his movements from behind the small window. He sniffed around the vegetable patch and dug a few holes but came up with nothing. Then he disappeared around the shed, so I had to creep out and peer behind it. There he was digging up another hole. He sniffed about in the hole, and that's when I saw him with something yellow in his mouth. Ha! I thought as I pounced on him from behind. Gandalf gave a yelp, and something bounced to my feet. It was the yellow rubber ball that had gone missing a few days before. No underwear yet. I spent all morning following our pup and searching in holes for the missing underwear in vain.

I was feeling very morose at lunch and even the chocolate cake Mum and Miranda had made tasted dry. I couldn't admit to Mum that she had been right about the underpants, and she would only get angry if she found that Gandalf had hidden or destroyed all of it. Not to mention Miranda, who would get into hysterics with the news.

I spent the whole weekend looking, and by Sunday evening I had come up with zilch. What was even more intriguing was that Miranda hadn't said anything to me about *her* missing underwear.

Poor girl, I thought, feeling sorry for my sister, which was quite out of character for me. That was how stressed out I was by Sunday night. If Miranda wasn't saying anything, then I certainly wouldn't. We couldn't let Mum find out about this. Then I had a brainwave.

I put the alarm clock on for six o'clock on Monday morning and decided I would use Gandalf to help me find the missing underwear. I took the only pair of underwear I had left from under the mattress and made Gandalf get a good sniff making sure he wouldn't grab at them with his teeth.

"Go Gandalf, go find the others!" I had seen a TV programme where people trained their dogs to find missing things or people. I was sure I could get Gandalf to niche out the underwear if he recognised the smell. Sure enough, he headed straight to the door and cocked his head, letting out a whimper. I crept to the door and opened it to let our pup out. I tiptoed behind Gandalf as he made his way along the landing.

To my surprise, instead of going downstairs, and out to the garden, he went up the stairs to the second floor where the study and the large attic was. This wasn't going to work I thought in desperation, but I followed as quietly as I could anyway. Gandalf disappeared up the stairs, and when I reached the second floor, he was sitting under the attic trap door looking up, and his tail wagging.

Now I was baffled. What was so exciting about the attic? Intrigued, I picked Gandalf up and pulled down the sliding ladder and climbed up carefully with Gandalf in my arms. No sooner had I opened the trap door that Gandalf bounced out of my hands and clambered over the cluttered objects towards a large chest. He jumped up on his forelegs and rested them on the chest, wagging his tail.

"You are a funny pup," I exclaimed, rubbing him under his chin and pushing him off the trunk, "How could you have possibly hidden the underwear here?" I chuckled and picked him up to go downstairs when Miranda's head popped up from the trap door.

"What are you doing here with Gandalf?" she exclaimed. "the whole point of putting them here was to keep him away from them!"

"What are you talking about? Keep him away from what?"

"From these of course," Miranda said scrambling up through the trap door and coming towards me.

She went up to the chest and opened the latch. She lifted the heavy lid with some effort, and it fell back with a thud.

There on top of a pile of fancy dress costumes were all my underwear and hers!

Grandpa and the Toffee Shop

"Jacob! Lily!" shouted grandpa from downstairs, "I'll treat you to our favourite shop."

"Yes!" I exclaimed, swivelling around on the floor expecting to meet my sister's twinkling eyes at the thought of one of those delicious toffees from the village's sweet shop.

Lily, who had been busy moving the tiny furniture about in her dollhouse just a moment before, was now singing a lullaby to Judy, her cherished rag doll and was lost in her own world. The dollhouse is one of Grandpa's incredible creations. He spends hours locked up in his fantastic shed at the back of the garden and often comes out with a surprise for either Judy or myself.

A mischievous idea came to me, and the more I thought about it, the more I assured myself it was only fair. Every time we went to the Toffee shop, Lily always seemed to get extras by putting on her sweet granddaughter act, and that really wasn't fair. It was time for retribution ...to call for a small solving of debts.

I watched her as she sang softly, and as she did, I also noticed her eyelids getting heavier and heavier. Taking advantage of this stroke of luck, I tiptoed ever so slowly out of the room and very, very gently closed the door behind me. I waited a few seconds, glueing my ear to the door to listen to any awakening noises. All was silent from inside. Lily had obviously fallen asleep.

When I went out to the garden gate to join Grandpa, I explained that Lily was fast asleep and I really couldn't wake her up, because she had been complaining of a stomach ache just an hour before. In fact, I recommended that we only get a few toffees for her, as it might give her an even worse tummy ache is she had too many toffees.

Grandpa looked a bit puzzled. "Asleep? At this time of the day? Oh well, I guess she isn't very well then. Maybe we should tell grandma before we go."

"Oh she was fine, uh, I mean she was sleeping soundly when I came downstairs, and I'm sure she'll be much better after a good nap. Although she really ought to avoid too many toffees," I hinted to my grandpa. So, off we headed to the toffee shop on the west side of the village.

When I heard the merry tinkle of the door and sniffed the delicious scent of the toffee blends as we walked into the toffee shop, I felt a tingling of delight. I couldn't wait to savour one of my favourite mint toffees and already imagined it melting slowly in my mouth. It was also one of Lily's favourite, I thought, feeling only mildly guilty. So, I headed to the huge jar on the left of the counter where the paper serving bags were hanging.

As I reached out for one of the bags, eager to plunge the large wooden serving spoon into the toffee jar, I heard a chiding voice behind me, "Oh, so you're the one who lies to his little sister then."

I looked up startled. I turned towards the counter from where the voice had come, then nervously glanced over at Grandpa. He was at the other end of the shop looking into another jar, but he seemed not to have heard.

Behind the counter stood an elderly lady, whom I had never seen before. She had a dark purple shawl on and her hair was tied up in a tight bun. She was looking at me with a mocking smile.

"Hmmm," I stammered. "I think you're confusing me with someone else."

Grandpa looked up at me from behind the large jar full of bright red and white humbug toffees. "Did you say something, Jacob?"

"Hem, no grandpa, just thinking out loud."

"Of course you are my boy," went on the old lady, "maybe you should think a little about sharing sweets too," she said frowning at me.

I tried to ignore her and started moving away from the counter and the jar. I peeped into another huge jar, next to the one my grandpa was looking at.

"That's right boy," sniggered the old lady eyeing me under her bushy white eyebrows. The more I looked at her, the more I swore she could have been Lily disguised as an old woman, wearing one of those old costumes our mother kept in the chest in the attic. She would sometimes use them for her pantomimes at school.

"Have a look at those strawberry toffees over there," went on the old woman," those are your sister's favourites I seem to remember."

Grandpa looked over at me with a frown. "Did you say something, Jacob?"

I shook my head vigorously without uttering a word.

I pulled out a strawberry toffee from the jar. I would chew on it myself later, whether or not it was Lily's favourite and I nearly screamed as I dropped it back in the jar. "Hands off you bag of lies, I'm Lily's toffee, not yours," squealed the toffee.

I started trembling and came closer to Grandpa, who looked at me puzzled again and said," Haven't you chosen any toffees yet my boy? Anyone would think you didn't like them from the look on your face."

He shook his head and went over to the other side of the shop where large drawers panelled with wood showcased special cream and chocolate toffees.

I felt as if all the toffees were watching me now, as well as the old lady behind the counter. She was definitely keeping a nasty eye on me, her mocking smile still plastered on her face. I decided to try the green square jar where the vanilla toffees were stored. I took a paper bag from another rack placed near the entrance and went to open the top of the jar. It was stuck. I pulled and pulled, but it just wouldn't budge. I was contemplating on whether to ask Grandpa for help, but when I looked up, I noticed the old woman was shaking her head ever so discreetly.

Well, forget that then I thought, not wanting her to say anything else about Lily out loud again. I went over to the drawers Grandpa was looking through and saw the fruit toffee section. But before I could open one of the drawers, I noticed a strange-looking label on the one I was about to open. *Hands off, this is Lily's toffee drawer!*

I stepped back aghast. This wasn't happening, my stomach started churning, and I felt sick to my stomach as a wave of guilt swept through me. Suddenly I didn't really fancy chewing on toffees at all.

I went up to Grandpa and whispered to him, not wanting the old lady to overhear. "Grandpa, I think I'm not feeling that good either, I guess I must be catching Lily's bug."

My grandpa turned around, a look of concern in his eyes. "Oh, poor boy, you don't look well at all. In fact, you look slightly green," he exclaimed.

Taking me by my arm, he went over to the counter and shook his head slightly at the elderly lady.

"I'm terribly sorry," he said, excusing himself," but I think my grandson isn't well. I'm afraid we'll have to skip the toffees this time."

"Oh dear," replied the lady with a twinkle in her eye, "I wonder what could have gotten over this young man. You look as if you've seen a ghost!"

"Yes," muttered my grandpa, apologetically, "terribly sorry Mr Mumble, we'll be back soon.

Once we were out of the toffee shop, I stared at my grandpa in disbelief. "Mr Mumble?" I asked taken aback, "That was more like Mr Mumble's old mother in there," I exclaimed puzzled.

Grandpa's white eyebrows shot up, and he bent over and peered into my eyes. "Dear, dear my boy, you aren't well, are you? Maybe you did see a ghost, after all. Make sure you don't tell your sister about it, she might get a fright."

"Oh I won't Grandpa, I won't," I replied with a shudder.

Great-Grandpa's Violin

Tara's Great Grandpa was a famous violinist, and everyone in the family played some musical instrument. Music floated about the house at all times of the day, and Tara adored her harmonious home and musical family. On Monday and Thursday afternoons, she would hear Mama's long tapered fingers fly over the black and white keys of the study's piano as she showed her students the mastery of the scales. Papa would get in late after work and, he too would head for the study to strum the nylon chords of his favourite acoustic guitar. While Toby, Tara's brother would shut himself up in the garden shed and bang on his drums for hours on end. Tara could nevertheless hear the rhythmic pounding as he beat his drumsticks on the hard surface of his drum set. The study was their music room. It wasn't one of those fabulously furnished ones with the latest hi-tech equipment. It had an old stand up piano and two guitars as well as an electric keyboard. The drum set was too cumbersome and loud to have in the study, so that went up in the garden shed. The only other classical instrument in the room was Great Grandpa's violin, and that was stowed away in a glass cabinet away from dust and light. It was precious, and no one was allowed to touch it, especially not Tara, who was known for her clumsiness.

Tara loved her musical family and her melodious home. She felt blessed with the gaiety of the music that enveloped her. However, there was one significant problem. Tara was the only one in her family who couldn't play an instrument.

Mother had sat next to Tara in front of the keys and patiently showed her the notes and the scales. But as much as Tara wanted to learn, she just couldn't seem to remember how the notes followed one another. Papa had done the same with his guitar, but that had been even more puzzling. Tara hadn't been able to get any tune to come out of Papa's guitar. All she could do was tweak the strings and get the same sound again and again. So they had finally given up on Tara. Her mother had shrugged and smiled. "I guess, you're just not musical my dear. There's nothing wrong with that." But Tara knew deep inside that she was 'musical', she had to be! She was sure that the music was somewhere within her hiding in a secret place.

On Tara's 8th birthday, they all gathered in the study to play some extra special music. The atmosphere was festive, and the music more enchanting than ever. Mama brought Tara's birthday cake into the study. She and Tara had worked on the icing decorations and had dotted the cake with musical notes made with coloured chocolate buttons. Even the candles were shaped like treble clefs. Tara adored everything about music, but as her family said, she was just not musical. They sang a happy birthday song with Mama drumming on the keys of the piano, and they all cheered and clapped as Tara blew out the candles.

"So what's your birthday wish this year?" asked Papa with a grin and a twinkle in his eyes.

Tara scrunched up her brow and stared at her family's smiling faces, and for the first time, she felt lonely. Here she was at her eighth birthday, with her loving family playing music to make her happy, but she suddenly felt she didn't belong. Maybe, she thought, Maybe I'm not musical because I'm not part of the family at all. What if they adopted me and they're keeping it a secret from me? Then everything would make sense. That's why I can't play the piano or the guitar. She gazed at the familiar faces again. They seemed frozen on the background of the study. Her eyes rested on the piano, then on the guitar and wandered towards the glass cabinet. Great Grandpa's violin seemed to gleam from behind the glass beckoning to her. Tara got up and went to stand in front of the cabinet staring at the sensuous contours of the shiny wooden surface. The bow was made of ivory and silver and was poised against the instrument.

"I would like to hold Great Grandpa's violin in my arms," Tara said in a faint voice.

Mama and Papa exchanged glances, and Papa gave Mama a small nod.

Papa took the keys to the cabinet which he kept in a small mother of pearl box on top of the piano and opened the glass door.

"Your Great Grandpa was one of the best violinists of the Kungliga Operan, the Royal Swedish Opera house," said Papa as he reached out to take the ancient instrument. He came over to Tara and sat her on his knee, and still holding the violin, he placed it into her arms.

"You don't remember, but Great Grandpa Elias used to sit you on his knee and play the violin when you were only one," said Papa, "unfortunately he died before you turned two and the violin has been there since then, as a reminder of what a great musician he was."

Tara lightly stroked the contours with her fingers and touched the rough strings. She felt them vibrate as her fingers followed the strings along the neck. The instrument seemed alive and ready to burst forth with a sweet melody that no one in her family had ever played.

That night Tara lay awake for a long time, thinking of Great Grandpa Elias's violin, and as she closed her eyes music rang in her ears. Not the clanging notes of the piano or the harmonious strumming of the guitar, but the sweet and floating notes of a classical air, she had never heard before.

She finally fell asleep and dreamt she was walking through a large doorway and entering an enormous inner hall. She found herself at the foot of a wide marble staircase with golden railings and all around her was the plush decor of a theatre. Then suddenly she was standing on a stage flooded with spotlights, and she could hear the murmur of the audience, then the hush before the beginning of the concert. Her stomach churned, and her heart beat faster. She turned sideways and next to her was a tall and imposing man with white hair and a warm smile. Immediately she knew this was her Great Grandpa Elias and she was in the Kungliga Operan. This was her big night, a night she would never forget. She was floating in this dreamlike atmosphere, through threads of music that drifted from the open dark oakwood doors — the musty odour of the wooden panelling and pungent aroma of the waxed floors tickled her nostrils. Tara was in a musical dreamland.

Tara and Elias played the violin together there in the opera house. Tara played for the first time, but it was as if she had played for years and her bow danced on the strings of her violin like magic fingers. When Tara and Elias finally reached the end she heard thunder. A deafening clapping filled her ears and tears flooded her eyes.

Tara woke up with a start. It was still dark outside but the moon was out, and Tara could clearly see the shed in the back of the garden. She sat up, wiping the tears from her eyes, and realised that she *was* part of the family. Very much so and she knew what she had to do now. She threw the duvet off her bed and tiptoed to her door then slowly opened it. The house was silent as it rarely was. She crept along the landing and down the stairs then into the study. The moonlight was filtering through the windows, and she could clearly see the guitars and the piano in the corner. She went over to the piano and opened the mother of pearl box, fished out a key and went over to the glass cabinet. The violin was shining behind the glass beckoning to her. She pushed a chair under the cabinet and climbed up on to it, turning the key in the lock of the cabinet door. Then gently, she reached out and took the violin and the bow. She sat down on the chair and fitted the violin under her chin as she had done in her dream, then ever so gently she pushed down the strings on the neck of the violin and touched the strings with the bow. She started ever so slowly, gaining in precision. Soon, the sweet melody that had rung in her ears on the stage of the opera house, floated around the study then out into the hall and up the stairs. The gentle tune filled the house in those early hours of the morning like an enchanting stream of happiness. Tara had found her musical talent at last. Her Great Grandpa Elias would have been proud of his great-granddaughter Tara.

The Binkfoy

Binkerdom was a far off realm in the kingdom of Ambledore. It was nestled in the extreme west of this harsh and barren territory and was the only strip of land blessed with verdant plant life and gushing natural springs. The rest of the kingdom was hostile and rugged, hard to harvest and desolate to live on.

Within the realm of Binkerdom, lay only lush plant life, an abundance of trees and thousands of different species of flowers, of an astounding broad spectrum of hues. There were no dwellings, no visible signs of settlements, just an expanse of green, thick woods and luscious flora.

However, there was one rootless presence within the realm. Neither plant, animal nor human in aspect and demeanour, but instead, a blend of all three. Lithesome and elegant in movement, amiable but aloof in manner. He was known as the Binkfoy.

The Binkfoy was a tall, reed-like figure, with green-hued skin and long slender limbs, wrapped with sinewy muscles, similar to tree roots that broke free from the ground to capture the surface. His hands were disproportionately large, with fingers bearing bulbous knuckles and long, incurved, dark blue nails. He walked with a gracious gait, his long hair flowing down like creepers from a tree. His face had chiselled features and a jutting chin, while his eyes gleamed like a pool of water in a grotto, reflecting the rare light filtering in from the outside world.

Now, although Binkerdom was part of the Ambledore Kingdom, it was independent of its laws. The Queen of Ambledore could not extend her powers over Binkerdom, and only the Binkfoy could dispose of this land rich in nature's most precious gifts. This was where you could find the only plantlife from which to survive.

However, the Binkfoy was not unwilling to share his fortune and allowed the Ambledorians their share of plants each year. They were allotted with a certain number and could exploit these in their kingdom as best they thought.

The people of the Ambledore Kingdom were very humble and mild at heart, and generally grateful to the Binkfoy's generosity. But the drudgery of the land led to an increasing feeling of discomfort and a sense of unfairness.

They were honest and kind-hearted, but it was hard to find the energy to struggle. Month after month, the people tended to their newly planted gardens in vain. Despite their efforts, these plants never survived, due to the harshness of the soil. Without fail at each try, the plants slowly shrivelled up and died, hardly providing fruit for one season.

One can imagine that the Ambledorians, although hardworking and patient, were tired of this life of sacrifice and misery. As time went by, they grew more and more disheartened, and increasingly envious of the Binkfoy's fortune.

So, within some households throughout Ambledore, families started plotting to find a way of getting more of their share of plants, in the hope of reaping better crop from the barren land. They also secretly complained of the fact that the Binkfoy himself did not feed on the plants he was the guardian of, and could, therefore, be more generous in his share of the plants.

They finally started meeting among families and laid down a plan to take over Binkerdom. Alas, the only way to do so, was to take the Binkfoy as a prisoner, and if worse came to the worst, he would have to be destroyed.

One moonless night, six of the more daring families gathered by Tumbledore Bridge, the last bridge crossing over the Ambledore River into Binkerdom. There were twenty of them, among the bravest of the men in the families, armed with ropes and spades, for they possessed no other weapons. They were optimistic about their mission and intended to capture the Binkfoy, without injuring him, for, after all, they were peaceful people.

The oldest and wisest man of the group was named Barold the Bold. He was sent forward with a message for the Binkfoy, asking him to allow the people of Ambledore access Binkerdom, as they needed food for their children, and more plants to grow and reap fruits from.

Barold found the Binkfoy resting in the recess of an ancient and large oak. He seemed to be expecting him, and was unruffled by Barold's words. The Binkfoy replied with unabated calmness that this was not possible. He was generous enough to provide them with the plants from his realm, they should, therefore, be content with those they were given.

A defeated Barold made his way back to the encampment by the bridge, to tell about the Binkfoy's unequivocal response. The other heads of the families grew angry and felt humiliated by such behaviour. It was therefore decided, on the spot, that he should be eradicated, for his behaviour was unjust and selfish.

The Ambledorians seemed to have forgotten that Binkerdom was not theirs to share at will. However, anger renders man blind to what is rightful or not. So, that night they went ahead and tainted their hands with the Binkfoy's blood. It gushed out emerald green from his wounds until his lithe body surrendered its last breath, under the thick canopy of his beloved trees. The Ambledorians cried out their victory and started rampaging this realm, source of life and beauty.

But lo and behold, although it was true that the Binkfoy did not feed on the plants he protected, little did the Ambledorians know that it was the plants that fed on him. The trees, plants and flowers grieved his loss.

He was the guardian of this enchanted and luscious realm, and without him, they could no longer survive. Binkerdom would slowly shrivel up and die, blending in with the Kingdom of Ambledore to become another strip of barren land, which would no longer bear flower, leaf or fruit.

Thus, the Ambledorians cried on their fate, on their greed, for those who seek too much are left with just a handful of dust. They were now doomed to perish, having destroyed their only life source. The Binkfoy.

The End of the Rainbow

Leila waited all afternoon, her chin resting on the window sill. She watched the dark clouds and followed the drops of rain with the tip of her finger as they slid down the window pane.

When would the sun come out?

She enjoyed the cosy feeling of being inside when it was cold and windy in the garden. Still, she loved the warm sun and the sweet scent of the garden flowers even more.

The clouds grew darker, and the rain drummed harder on the glass pane, merging the drops into one long river.

Leila shivered and hugged her one-eyed teddy. She stroked Teddy to comfort him and whispered, "Don't worry, the sun will soon come out and with it ... the rainbow."

Leila and Teddy waited, and as they waited, their eyelids grew heavy. Slowly eyelashes touched eyelashes cradled by the soft pitter-patter of the raindrops, and the morning gave way to the afternoon.

Warm fingers caressed Leila's brow and the heat spread across her face, reaching her nose, lips and chin. Her eyes fluttered open, and for a moment, she was blinded by the rays of the afternoon sun. The dark clouds were running away in the distance beaten by the wind and the sun's glowing tentacles.

Suddenly, right in front of her, beyond the garden, the rainbow started to appear.

First came violet, followed by indigo, Leila's favourite colour. Next came blue, green and then yellow came bursting out like a ray of golden sun. Leila held her breath as she waited for the last two colours. She clutched Teddy tightly and stared so hard that the rainbow blurred and seemed ready to disappear again. Teddy's only eye was about to pop out with all the squeezing when finally, orange and red materialized side by side next to the yellow.

"Quick Teddy, let's follow the rainbow before it fades away. We have to find the end of the rainbow."

Leila had heard many stories about rainbows, but she was sure they were all old wives tales. She was going to find out for herself.

Dragging Teddy by a tattered arm, she opened her bedroom door a crack. Leila craned her head around the door to make sure no one was about to stop her on her quest. She was sure her mum would never let her go out in the muddy garden. The only way to get to the garden was to sneak out. Creeping along the landing, she listened for the familiar noises coming from the study and tiptoed down the stairs. Once in the kitchen, she slipped on her rubber boots and anorak and inch by inch, she opened the kitchen door that led into the garden.

The fresh evening air was damp and warm as she inhaled. A blackbird popped out from under the shelter of a bush. Hop, hop, squee, squee. Leila would have stopped to watch the friendly bird, but today she had to hurry, she had to follow the rainbow to the end.

She looked up, afraid it had vanished. But there it was in all its glory the seven colours glowing so vividly that Leila reached out to touch it. Her fingers met with a branch heavy with cold droplets that sprinkled her brown curls.

She giggled and hurried to the garden gate towards the rainbow. She ran out of the gate, leaving it hanging on its hinges, and into a field that dipped gently into a valley bejewelled with clover. When Leila stepped onto the pink and white carpet, a sweet vanilla scent filled her nostrils. The clover flowers whipped around Teddy as Leila skipped down the valley towards the river and the rainbow.

"It's diving into the river," shouted Leila to the birds and the wind. "Quick before it goes underwater and vanishes again!"

The colours of the rainbow were now glowing intensely. The red reminded Leila of the flames in the November bonfires, but as she reached the end of the slope, the colours seemed to fade. Leila ran faster and faster. The end of the rainbow was getting closer, but its colours were a hazy blur merging with the waters of the river.

Leila jumped on to the old wooden bridge that crossed the bubbling waters and was suddenly enveloped in a thick mist.

A million droplets of frost sparkled around her, like frozen fireflies in a spiralled dance. Some tickled her nose while others brushed past her ears. She smelt something peculiar, which reminded her of the earth and sea all at once. The haze intensified and she could no longer see the other side of the riverbank, but, here, the colours of the rainbow glowed so intensely that Leila had to shield her eyes. She stretched out her arm to touch the red but only saw Teddy clutched in her hand. Then, just as it had appeared, the red faded, followed by the orange, yellow, green, and blue. Her favourite colour indigo disappeared, then came back to say goodbye for a few seconds, and took the violet away with it.

Now, even the frosted fireflies had stopped dancing. The fun had ended, the rainbow had left the scene. Leila's head dropped, and she hugged Teddy to comfort him.

From an eyelash, a tear sprung and spattered Teddy's head. Then eyelashes met eyelashes.

Maybe, just maybe, if she closed her eyes, the rainbow would come again, and this time she would follow it to the end.

The First Winter

Jabari had always been a courageous kid. When his mother was alive, she used to tell him that he was the only baby in the village not to cry when the fierce storms whipped at the huts and the thunder shook the earth with a mighty rumble.

Jabari meant 'the brave one' in the Bankonjo dialect. But Jabari wasn't feeling brave at all. He was scared and lonely. The Bankonjo village belonged to a fading dream, and Jabari had woken up in another world.

The alien fields and woods that lay before his dark eyes were desolate and colourless.

The plains in the Semuliki Valley had always been verdant and the trees luxurious, their branches heavy with leaves. Jabari's feet were hard and calloused due to the scorching earth he had walked on for the past seven years.

Now he was trembling as frosty fingers brushed the bronze skin of his round face, and icy needles pierced through the uncomfortable sneakers he was wearing.

All around him the grass was yellow and the branches carried no leaves at all.

Jabari had never imagined that such a place could exist. An inhospitable land where icy winds and barren landscapes were the only scenery for miles on end.

Jabari had returned to the village one evening from a three-day fishing expedition with his two elder brothers to find their village razed to the ground. Spirals of smoke rose silently from the blackened huts and rubble, while strange people clad in white roamed around like ghosts in the smoky mist. Jabari had been deadened with shock, staring at the deserted village before him. Then the lady with the ashen face had come and knelt beside him taking his honey-brown hand. She had whispered odd words mixed with the Bankonjo dialect. Right away, Jabari knew he could trust the stranger with the green eyes speckled with grey. He had gone with her leaving his brothers and the phantom village behind.

Jabari knew she would take care of him just as his mother had. But now, he was scared. Why had she brought him here, to this hostile place?

A hand rested on his frail shoulder, the same hand that had taken his in the faraway plains of the Semuliki Valley.

"It's winter Jabari," came a gentle voice from behind him, "Here, we have four seasons. Spring is my favourite. The temperature gets warmer, and the blossoms burst from the branches with pinks, whites, yellows and reds. Flowers paint the green fields with a palette of bright colours. Then comes summer when the sun is nearly as hot as it was in the village where you were born. You wait. We'll soon swim in the lake and snooze under the canopy of the oak trees."

Jabari wondered what she meant. There were no leaves on the trees here. Why didn't the leaves just stay on the trees all the time, and why was it so cold? He liked the thought of colourful flowers and wondered if they would be bell-shaped like the ones in the forest near his village.

The soft voice soothed his agitation. "Then comes autumn when the first chill wafts across the land from the north. The leaves fade and turn yellow, brown, orange, and even purple. The wind blows hard, and the leaves get carried away from the trees and settle on the ground for the winter.'"

Jabari didn't like the sound of the harsh wind tearing the leaves off the branches. Maybe he could say a prayer and ask God to stop the evil storm from destroying the leaves. Jabari wasn't afraid of the storm. He was scared of the desolation. The storms in the village had never ripped the trees bare from all their leaves, but this wind was bad. It took everything away with it.

"Finally, winter comes. This is the time Nature sleeps and regenerates, and the animals take shelter in their burrows and dens. It's such a peaceful time of the year."

Jabari shivered. How long would the animals hide for? Would the fish bury themselves under the silt at the bottom of the lake? He wanted to go fishing again like he had done with his brothers. What was so lovely and peaceful about the grey and frozen land before them?

Another hand touched Jabari's other shoulder, and now the gentle voice was close to his ear.

"Close your eyes Jabari and smell the air. Can you sense something different?"

Jabari closed his eyes and sniffed. His nostrils tingled as droplets of frost shot up his nose. The air was still and silent and felt less hostile now that his eyes had blocked out the dreary scenery.

Jabari remained silent with his eyes closed for a few minutes, then started to fidget.

"Be patient Jabari, soon very soon, you'll see how wonderful winter can be."

Jabari, couldn't imagine anything beautiful about desolate fields and trees void of their emerald ornaments. Still, he waited, feeling the comfort of the reassuring hands on his shoulders, and the warm breath as the voice whispered in his ear.

Suddenly, Jabari felt something tickle his nose, then his eyelid. It was strangely warm and cold at the same time. It brushed his cheek then the other, and the tip of his ear. He tasted something fresh and prickly on his lips. The atmosphere was shrouded in complete silence, yet was charged with magnetic energy.

Jabari could no longer wait for the voice to tell him he could open his eyes. His eyelashes fluttered open, shaking off something heavy and wet.

"This, Jabari is winter."

Jabari opened his mouth, but no words escaped. A tiny white flake dropped and melted on his tongue, then another. All around him, little bundles of cotton, like the ones he used to pick with his mother, fell from the sky and settled over the bare land. They covered the dry grass, the barren branches, and the brown shrubs. A layer of pure white cotton formed on his bristly black hair. He touched his head and tried to pluck off the cotton. It felt soft and cold, and when he looked into the palm of his hand, he saw the cotton disappear, leaving a small puddle of droplets.

Jabari turned around his eyes wide with amazement searching the green eyes speckled with grey.

Then the most wonderful thing happened. The green eyes smiled and filled with joy. The lady with the ashen face hugged him hard for the first time, and Jabari felt a warmth he hadn't felt in a long time.

"This, Jabari is snow," she said as she held him close against her heart. They stood there for a long time, while the snowflakes came floating down from the sky laying on and all around them, glowing like pearl drops. Jabari opened his mouth and waited for the snowflakes to fall onto his tongue, so he could taste the freshness of winter. Winter no longer seemed barren and cruel. It wasn't an enemy like the fire that had taken away his family and village, leaving him cold and empty inside. Winter carried the snow, which was soft and harmless and purified his heart from all the sadness he had been too afraid to voice.

He silently said a prayer, wishing that winter would never end and the warm embrace would continue forever.

The Hot Air Balloon

I had heard of car races, of horse races, bicycle races, boat races and even of dog races. But never in my life had I come across a hot balloon race. In fact, I had never seen a hot air balloon in my life!

I know about plenty of things because I have lots of books about many different subjects on the shelves in my bedroom. Still, somehow I had missed out on hot air balloons. So, I went to look them up as soon as my uncle told me about the race. I didn't want to show him I was totally uninformed. But I had to go to the library because I couldn't find that particular book on my bedroom shelves, nor in the downstairs study.

When I entered the huge municipal library, which is quite a walk from our house, a white-haired lady sitting at the reception counter eyed me from behind round spectacles. Without asking me what I was looking for, she pointed to the right and nodded. I shrugged and followed the directions without further questions.

Of course, she had sent me to the children's section, and that was not where I wanted to be. One by one, I read all the shiny plated signs on the enormous bookcases. Fiction, Non-fiction, Geography, Arts and Crafts, History and Science... I wondered where the books about hot air balloons could possibly be. I didn't want to ask the lady at the reception desk, she hadn't seemed very friendly.

It took me ages to find the book I wanted, and by that time, my tummy was rumbling, and I was getting tired. My eyes rested on the top shelf of the history section.

'The History of Hot Air Ballooning.' I pulled down the heavy book from the shelf and settled down on one of the giant cushions in the children's section.

I opened the book and started reading. Hot air ballooning was the oldest form of aviation in history, and it all started over two hundred years ago. A French scientist sent a duck, a sheep and a cockerel up in the first-ever hot air balloon. I chuckled to myself, imagining the poor frightened animals. After that, several other scientists and adventurers from France, England and Italy started doing test flights. This time they went up themselves, sometimes with their animal friends too. I paused and wondered why they took the animals in the first place. Then in 1785 an American and a French finally crossed the Channel for the first time and delivered the first-ever airmail letter.

My eyelids were getting heavier and heavier, and I settled down more comfortably in the soft cushion.

"Wake up, boy!" Someone was shaking me awake, but I felt so drowsy I could hardly hear the voice. It seemed to come from ever so far.

"Wake up! Where's the food hamper I asked you to bring over to the gondola?"

I eventually managed to open my eyes. A man with a beard and an odd-looking hat formed like a bowl was frowning down at me. I looked around frantically. Gone were the cushions and the books. I seemed to be in a sort of stable sitting against a large basket.

Another man came striding in, he too wore a hat, but this one I recognised as a top hat. Both men were dressed in suits and silk cravats, but not of the kind my uncle wears when he goes to the opera twice a year.

"Come on quick!" said the second man in a strange accent, "the envelope is full of gas and ready for departure!" He was holding a spaniel on a leash and knelt down to pat the spaniel fondly.

"You get the hamper John, and the boy can hold Archie, while we set the gauges and prepare for flight."

For flight? What were these men talking about? But before I could ask, Archie pulled me up and dragged me out into the blare of the morning sun.

An enormous crowd had gathered around the most incredible spectacle I had ever laid eyes on. It wasn't just a regular hot air balloon of the kind you see nowadays, with colours and fancy sponsors sprawled all over the balloon part. This was something else. Something quite extraordinary.

The balloon was not oblong-shaped but more rounded, and it had a netting draped over it with hundreds of strings attached to a large ring at the base of the balloon. More strings hung from the ring and were secured to a wicker basket shaped like a bathtub with feet. While wing-shaped oars jutted from the sides and were lined in what looked like silk. The large envelope was floating above the wicker base swinging slightly from left to right. Inside the odd-looking base was a burner from which a bluish flame was blazing right under the hole of the envelope.

"Pierre, check the gauges!" cried out the man named John who had clambered into the balloon's basket, "and you boy get into the gondola with Archie. Grab that anchor before you get in."

Too stunned to reply I picked up the heavy anchor and took it to the side of the gondola, which was obviously the name of the funny-looking base and heaved it over the side. Archie jumped up on the wicker and John pulled him in.

"Come on, boy, what are you waiting for, get in. We have no time to lose the envelope is full and hot and ready to soar!"

Before I knew it, I was in the gondola and Pierre, threw a second anchor in the gondola, jumped in and shouted to another assistant still on the ground.

"Cut the ropes!"

The crowd cheered and shouted as the gondola lurched back towards the ground then up with a sudden jerk and ascended swiftly up to the sky. The roar of the crowd grew fainter and fainter as the people gradually became dots on a background of green and brown patches.

The only sound was the hissing of the flame as it heated the enormous balloon over our heads.

"How are the gauges John?' asked Pierre in his thick accent. "You boy check the ropes for any damage." He nodded towards me and winked.

"We're making history today! You're the youngest man ever to fly in a balloon. and you, Archie the first animal!"

"The first, but not the only one," retorted John with a grin. He put his hand in the inside pocket of his elegant jacket and pulled out something furry with white and brown patches. A hamster! "Meet Agnus, our fifth passenger and our mascot for the flight!"

Archie sniffed at Agnus suspiciously, then wagged his tail.

"We are quite a crowd, " said John with a frown, "I hope this won't be a problem when we're over the sea."

Over the sea! I nearly shouted out loud. And before I could ask the obvious question, Pierre answered it for me. "Ah, la Manche, the Channel is in sight, my friends.

We're about to be the first humans and animals to cross the famous stretch of water."

All was silent for a while, apart from the hiss of the burner. The breeze was chilly, but the heat from the burner made the temperature around us warm. The fields below stretched peacefully, then rose on to the cliffs where white dots grazed on the pastures. Suddenly a flock of wild geese flew past in a V-formation, honking as they overtook the peculiar flying ship. All three of us gazed in awe at the spectacle below and around us too mesmerised to speak. Before we knew it, we were floating over the blue expanse, sparkling with gems of green, white and grey. I turned around and admired the chalk-white cliffs as they slowly withdrew from my view, glaring white and pure in the sunlight.

My stomach lurch as the gondola dropped from under our feet. "Quick, John, turn up the burner," cried Pierre.

"It's at its maximum," cried out John, "we're too heavy, we have to throw something overboard.

Without preamble, Pierre tossed the picnic hamper I was supposed to have been responsible for, out of the gondola. So much for our lunch, I thought. Then followed an anchor. The gondola seemed to stabilise and rise slightly.

"If I can get this propeller to work properly, we could gather up some forward motion. The wind is taking us off course," said John manoeuvring the large awkward-shaped paddle. It seemed useless to me and was probably weighing down the balloon too.

As if on cue, John detached the propeller from the gondola and threw it overboard.

"There go two months of hard work," said John with a groan.

"Well, John, if it doesn't work, it's no good to us is it?" said Pierre clapping his colleague friend on his back, " We need to get across whatever it takes!"

Slowly we made our way across the waters followed by miniature sails scattered across the blue expanse. My stomach grumbled, and I must have dozed off again because I was abruptly shaken awake by another jolt. I pulled myself up and clutched at the side of the gondola. I could now see the vast sandy beaches of the coast of France. But the sea looked much too close. We were losing height!

"Throw out the other anchor," shouted John to Pierre, and that equipment you always insist on bringing."

"But it's essential for our flight," rebuked Pierre.

"Nothing's essential if we crash into the Channel and drown. Away with all unnecessary material!"

John turned around and looked at me, and for a moment, I was terrified he would throw me out too. But he was looking at Archie.

"Here Archie boy. You'll have to abandon ship and me as well possibly." John then fished a strange-looking parachute from a large sack and attached it to Archie. He tightened the buckles and patted the dog good-bye. He hung the poor Archie overboard as he struggled to get free, then he let him go. I screamed in shock, not wanting to look.

Pierre started guffawing and slapped me on the back. "Look what fun Archie's having," he said between peals of laughter. Sure enough, Archie was hanging from his parachute sailing gently down towards the boats that were following our flight across the sea.

The gondola shuddered again and rose, then dropped lower again. The beaches were not far ahead, but the hot air balloon kept falling. John and Pierre were now frantically throwing whatever they could lay hands on overboard until all that was left were two men in just their shirts and underwear, myself and Angus, as well as a mailbag.

We were still dropping and gliding towards the coast, the water rushing dangerously near below us. I could now clearly see the surf of the waves and could hear the shouting from the sailing boats below. In a final strategic manoeuvre, Pierre pulled out the last of his desperate tricks. A parachute, he quickly donned it and was about to jump when miraculously the gondola reached the sandy expanse of the first French beach and glided over the golden powder. With a violent thump, the bathtub shaped basket hit the sand, and the envelope above swung lazily from left to right.

John and Pierre roared with triumphant cries and danced up and down in the gondola hugging each other. Then they picked me up and tossed me up and down. "Hurray, Hurray! We made it! We crossed the Channel, we made history!"

Up and down they tossed me until I felt dizzy, so dizzy and again they rocked and rocked me.

"Wake up, young man!" came a strange voice. I opened my eyes, expecting to see John. But it wasn't John this time. It was the white-haired lady staring at me from behind her spectacles. "This is a library, not a dormitory," she said with a frown. "Are you going to take that book out with you or not? It's nearly closing hour."

I got up and shook my head vigorously. "No thank you, ma'am, I think I've learnt enough from the book, I'll put it straight back."

I returned the book back on the shelf and walked out of the library into the setting sun. I sure had learnt a lot about hot air balloons, probably more than I had expected.

The Kindergarten Scissors

My teacher is a skinny, slightly hook-nosed lady, with a thick black bun of hair tightly pinned to the back of her narrow head. Now, any other kid, apart from my classmates and me, would no doubt be terrorized to have to weather hours of English, Maths and History under the scrutiny of such a teacher. But, we are a brave bunch, and we work diligently, trying to convince each other that these chilling features are really quite normal.

However, more than once, while I daydream in class, which rarely happens, of course... I slip a side glance at Mrs Cackle, and can you imagine what I see? Well, if I was sure you were as courageous as our class is, I might even begin to describe what happens ... or maybe not.

Nevertheless, I will provide you with some blander details, more suitable for those with weaker hearts.

Sometimes, I actually see the hairpins in Mrs Cackle's bun pop out! Her black hair frees itself from its trap and starts swirling around like an octopus' purple tentacles clouded in black ink. Such an unsettling image, to put it mildly. You can imagine how that makes me sit up and concentrate more on the lesson.

Once, something very extraordinary happened to Mrs Cackle's pointer. She really likes pointers, and has a bunch of really intriguing ones, in all odd shapes and sizes. I can't imagine where she finds such a collection. That day, she had her sharp wooden pointer, the one with strange swirly engravings near the handle. She was pointing it at me, when it suddenly started to wriggle like a worm, then it grew longer and longer, slipped from her hand on to the desk, taking the form of a black and emerald striped snake. I nearly shrieked out and jumped onto my desk. But no one else seemed to notice, so I took ten deep breaths, hid my head in the maths exercise book, and finished all the exercises in no time.

Another time, during an especially long and difficult Math test, one of my classmates 'unintentionally took a peek at his neighbour's paper. Mrs Cackle stared at him so intensely that her green eyes popped right out of their orbits like one of those funny characters in cartoons my sister and I watch after school. Tom nearly fell off his chair in fright. He grabbed his pencil that had fallen on the floor and buried himself in the test paper, never once looking up until the end of the test.

Now, this one is the weirdest. I was fishing in my pencil case for a pencil sharpener because the tip of my pencil had broken yet again. Why is it my pencils always need sharpening I wonder? As I fumbled through its contents, I came across my younger sister's kindergarten scissors. You know which ones I mean. Those silly rounded ones that can't even cut straight, let alone around edges!

I was scratching my head, wondering how they could have possibly jumped in there when the scissors started to snap at me. I leapt back getting away from them just in time. The scissors went wild and sliced away in a frenzy, shredding the pages of my history book. I was in a real state of panic, and I could feel Mrs Cackle's eyes boring into me with anger. Frantically, I tried to catch those crazy kindergarten scissors. Still, they kept slipping from my fingers and snapping away on a wild hunt. They were already half-way through the history book when they suddenly stopped in mid-air and dropped with a 'plonk' on the floor beside my desk.

I heaved a sigh of relief and opened my history book to check on the damage. As luck would have it the last page the scissors had lashed through was just before the one we were working on. I gratefully started reading at lightning speed, wondering how on earth I was going to stick all the previous pages back together. I would surely need rolls and rolls of tape for the task. At least the lesson was saved! I would certainly talk about the scissors with my sister and ask her where she had found them. Next, I would make her come with me to the back garden and bury them as deep as we could dig!

Looking back on all these strange happenings; believe me, I have spared you from the worst, somehow our class seems to get all their work done obediently and on time. Mrs Cackle must be a good teacher after all, if not somewhat disquieting. I wonder how she manages to make us work so well?

The Lady in the Moon

"Look! You can see the Man in the Moon," cried out Jacob with glee. The evening was warm, and the breeze carried with it the scent of honeysuckle and freshly mowed grass. A cricket chirped softly in the darkness, welcoming the beginning of summer.

Jacob and his older brother Tom were stretched out on the grass staring at the Moon above them. Jacob adored his older brother, who was six years older than him and knew everything about anything.

"That's what most people say," Tom said, "but not many know the truth."

Jacob lifted himself up on an elbow and stared at Tom's silvery silhouette looming up from the darkness.

"What'd you mean, the truth?"

Tom didn't stir. His arms were stretched out behind him, and his head was resting in the palms of his hands. He remained silent for a few minutes. Then he spoke ever so softly.

"I'm not sure you're ready for the truth baby brother. Very few know the secret behind who really lives in the Moon."

Jacob took a deep breath and inhaled the dampness of the grass. He held his breath for a few seconds, then blurted out, "I'm not a baby anymore. I can keep a secret now."

As soon as the words were out, Jacob felt his face go all hot. He was grateful that the dark shadows hid his bright red face. He hoped Tom wouldn't remember the time he had accidentally told Mum that Tom had sneaked out the window at night until dawn.

The night grew silent, and the warm breeze carried a chilly trail of humidity in its wake. Even the cricket had ended its song.

"Alright then," said Tom breaking the silence, "but don't go telling Mum I told you."

Jacob blushed again. Tom *did* remember. Jacob ignored the subtle rebuke, and replied, "I promise, I won't. You can trust me *now*."

"Close your eyes and open them only when I tell you it's OK," said Tom.

Jacob nodded in silence and settled down on his back again, feeling the damp grass through his cotton T-shirt. He squeezed his eyes shut and waited. A shiver of apprehension passed through his body. What could the secret be?

Then Tom revealed the secret. He told Jacob that the Man in the Moon wasn't a man at all, but a woman.

"They say it's a legend, but that's only because they don't want people to know that it's the truth. The Chang'e, the Goddess of the Moon is up there, not the Man, and I'll show you. Now open your eyes, very, very slowly. Look at the top right side of the Moon. Can you see her dark hair gathered up over her head and fastened with a white rose? Now follow an imaginary line down past her forehead and trace her nose and chin. Can you see her looking upwards towards the heavens?"

Suddenly there she was, in all her beauty. Her face was so vivid that Jacob wondered how he could possibly not have seen her before. She was beautiful, her pale skin was as delicate as the petals of a garden rose, and her hair as black as the night sky. Jacob stared in awe as he listened to his brother tell the story.

A very long, long time ago in an ancient province of China, autumn was approaching, and the leaves were gradually turning from green to red, yellow, purple, and brown. The people in the villages were harvesting before the winter when one morning, not one sun, but ten suns rose over the fields and crops. You can imagine what happened next. The suns shone day after day. Without a cloud to shelter the people and crop from the scorching suns, the land around the villages started to burn, and the precious harvest shrivelled and disintegrated.

Ths heat was so intense that even the earth was blistering and the water sizzled and evaporated from the wells. Fortunately for the villagers, there lived a famed archer in their Province. His name was Hou Yi. The Queen of the Province had him called to her court and begged him to use his skill and courage and save the land from the ten blazing suns, or the people would die.

Hou Yi was not just an excellent archer, he was also astute. He knew that he would have to shoot the suns right in their centre if they were to explode and disintegrate into the heavens. He also figured that he would have to wait until the light from the suns was less intense to be able to look directly at them and aim just right.

So the young Yi took his bow and arrows and waited until sunset. He dipped the tips of the arrows in tar and put fire to them. Then, he stretched the taut string of his bow as far as he could. One by one, he shot nine of the suns right in the centre just as they were setting over the horizon. When the last of the suns was about to sink behind the arid land, he put down his bow and let it descend untouched.

The villages in the provinces feasted and praised the brave Yi for weeks and gave birth to what is known today as the Mid-autumn festival. Yi became a hero, hailed as the saviour of the Province.

The Queen, grateful for his heroic deed, gave Hou Yi a precious gift. She presented him with the elixir of immortality. If he drank this potion, he would become a god and instantly ascend to heaven.

Now, as much as Hou Yi appreciated his gift, he was not sure he wanted to go to heaven. The truth is he was in love with the beautiful Chang'e. So he thanked the Queen and hid the magic potion, safely in his hut.

Soon after Yi married Chang'e. She too fell in love with Yi because of his kind nature and heroic disposition. They lived happily for the first month until something dreadful happened at the Queen's court.

One of the Queen's counsellors was banished from the palace, because he was caught stealing from the Queen. He was lucky that the Queen was kind-hearted or he would have lost his head for treason. Fengmeng was furious with the Queen who had left him destitute and shunned by the people. But he knew of the secret elixir, and he also knew where he could find it. He just hoped that Yi hadn't already used the potion for himself.

Yi had not. He had given it to Chang'e to keep. He loved her deeply and would only take the potion if he knew for sure that he could be with his beloved wife forever.

Meanwhile, the rascal Fengmeng spied on Yi's house, and when he was ready, he waited for Yi to leave the house on one of his hunting trips. As soon as Yi was no longer visible in the far distance, Fengmeng broke into the house and forced Chang'e to reveal the safe place of the potion. He threatened her with a knife and told her he would kill her if she didn't hand the elixir over. At that very moment, Chang'e knew she had no other choice. She opened a small casket hidden in a trunk where her husband stored his bows and arrows, and carefully pulled out the crystal bottle. But before Fengmeng could grab it from her, she drank the potion in one gulp to prevent the crook from using it to hurt or exploit the people of the Province.

Suddenly Chang'e was enveloped in a golden glow, and a voice whispered to her asking her where, in the heavens, she would prefer to live. She chose the Moon as her home, which was the closest place to her husband, whom she loved dearly. So Chang'e who took her husband's place in the Moon.

Yi never told the Queen what had happened for fear she would be angry with him. He spent the rest of his nights sleeping outside in the field regardless of the season. And when the night was clear as this one is, husband and wife would talk and sing together. They loved each other dearly until Yi's death. The lady in the Moon still sings to him on clear nights. If you're very quiet and the crickets stop chirping, you can just make out the silvery notes.

Jacob closed his eyes and reached out for Tom's hand in the darkness. With the cool night breeze came a faint humming, so sweet it plunged Jacob into a dream world of rolling hills painted yellow, orange, red and purple.

The Lion's Mane

Jayden loved to explore the woods. They stretched over the rise from the foot of the hill where the village lay, just outside Grandpa's doorstep. Jayden and Grandpa used to take long walks on summer afternoons and collect all sorts of herbs and strange-looking roots. Grandpa would prepare herbal teas using the flowers and leaves of thyme and add a generous teaspoon of honey and give it to Jayden to drink. Although it took some time for Jayden to get used to the taste, he had learnt to enjoy the fuming magic potion, which regularly got rid of his allergy cough.

Grandpa's kitchen smelt deliciously of wood, herbs and spices. They were stored everywhere. In large glass jars, hanging in bunches from strings, crushed to powder and kept in small tin boxes; wherever you turned to in the cluttered kitchen, you would find a dried out plant to cure all sorts of aches and illnesses.

Today Grandpa was not in the kitchen as was his custom, rummaging in the small wooden drawers over the sink, or mixing his concoctions to make infusions and pastes. He was in bed, resting.

Mama had not wanted Jayden to stay for the weekend with Grandpa. She said he was too weak to look after an eight-year-old boy. But Jayden had insisted that he could look after himself very well thank you. Besides, Grandpa needed his company to get better. His mother reluctantly agreed, and she had prepared a few dishes to take to Grandpa's house. The two of them could easily heat them over the old Aga stove whenever they were hungry.

Mama was usually happy about Jayden staying with Grandpa. The only sweet things hidden in Grandpa's kitchen cupboards were cinnamon and nutmeg and occasional homemade gingerbread biscuits. The single goody Grandpa had learnt from Grandma's panoply of baking recipes.

Before Mother left, she covered Grandpa's knees with what had been Grandma's favourite hand-knit blanket.

"Now you two behave, and you Grandpa don't even think of getting up to wander in the woods."

"And don't forget the pills the doctor prescribed," she shouted, walking out of the front door.

Jayden watched his mother through the window as she got in the family car and slammed the door. His hazel eyes flecked with green followed the red car as it sped down the path and out of the open gate towards the village.

He spun around and grinned at Grandpa, but his grin instantly faded. Grandpa had fallen asleep in the armchair.

For as long as Jayden remembered, Grandpa had never napped during the day. Jayden's tummy contracted, and he gulped down a lump in his throat.

Jayden tiptoed out of the kitchen to unpack his overnight bag when he heard Grandpa's voice from the kitchen. "Where are you tiptoeing to my boy? Were you going to play a trick on your lazy Grandpa?"

Jayden leapt back into the kitchen with a radiant smile. "You were sleeping. I didn't want to bother you. Mama told me the doctor said you should get as much rest as possible."

"Nonsense! It's those dratted pills he gave me. All they do is make me fall asleep. The pain in my legs is still as bad as ever when I walk," grumbled Grandpa. "But if only we could..."

"What?" asked Jayden, intrigued, "what could we do?"

"We could prepare a special potion that would get me on my feet again."

"Well, let's do it! What are we waiting for Grandpa?"

"This time it's not that easy; this concoction is not like any other we have made before. We need a very special ingredient from the woods."

Jayden was so thrilled that he couldn't stop jumping about. A potion that could get Grandpa walking again!

"Don't get too excited. It's not just any herb we can easily pick in the woods. It is a rare mushroom that grows in the deepest part of the woods. You can only spot it just before dawn. If you're very lucky."

It all sounded very mysterious to Jayden, and he was starting to get the jitters.

"This particular mushroom is called Lion's mane because it looks a bit like the mane of a lion. It grows in a single clump at the base of the oldest oaks in the woods and has dangling spines like fringes."

Grandpa told Jayden that he had only found it once in his whole life when he was very young and his eyes were quick and alert.

Jayden wanted to prove to Grandpa that he was brave and as alert as his Grandpa had been, and more than anything he wanted Grandpa to get better.

"If you help me along, we can go together, and with my nose and your eyes, we could no doubt find the Lion's Mane. Of course, we wouldn't tell your mother. She would say I'm a crazy old man walking in the woods at night with my eight-year-old grandson. But it would be fun, wouldn't it?" He added with a wink, his pale blue eyes twinkling with mischief.

So Jayden and Grandpa set off an hour before dawn towards the woods. The going was slow. Grandpa had to lean on Jayden and stop every few steps to rest. Jayden could tell he was in great pain although he didn't once complain. Beads of sweat had formed on Grandpa's forehead despite the chilly air. They finally arrived at the edge of the woods, and Grandpa sat down on a large stone too exhausted to take another step.

"I don't think I can make it into the woods. I would probably trip and fall, and then we would be in real trouble. We'll just have to go back after I've rested here a while."

Jayden was shattered. He had been so enthusiastic about getting the Lion's mane. Once they had found it, Grandpa would be up and walking as before. They had got this far. He wasn't going to turn back without the magic mushroom.

"I'll go, Grandpa," said Jayden clenching his jaws, "I'll find the Lion's Mane."

Grandpa suppressed a smile. "It doesn't matter, boy. I'll take the pills the doctor gave me. The pain in my legs will just take a little longer to go away."

"Grandpa, you've made it all the way up the hill, you're not going to give up now."

Jayden was trying to convince himself as he talked to Grandpa. He didn't want to show Grandpa that he was scared to go into the dark woods.

Grandpa was silent for a few moments. Jayden could feel his pale blue eyes piercing the darkness. "You've never been in the woods alone Jayden. However, the woods are peaceful and enchanting, if dark and mysterious. But, most of all they are friendly and no threat to us at all. They nourish the animals, provide shelter and even wood to burn. Do you hear me, Jayden?"

Jayden nodded. Grandpa's words gave him courage.

"When you get to the middle of the woods, where the largest oaks grow, wait until the first rays of dawn. It shouldn't be long now, so you had better hurry. You will find the Lion's Mane at the base of the oldest oak trees on the side facing the east. And remember Jayden, the animals of the woods are our friends. Never underestimate the wisdom of the woods."

Jayden nodded in the silent night. It wasn't really that dark. He could clearly see Grandpa's features.

But when he entered the woods and started following the familiar dirt path, the darkness swallowed him up like a giant monster.

The woods were eerily silent. The thud of his steps on the soft ground echoed ominously. Occasionally he stepped on a fallen branch, and it cracked loudly, making him flinch. He wanted to avoid waking up any of the bigger animals. Something scurried past on his right, and he nearly jumped out of his skin.

Step by step, he went deeper into the woods, picking up more and more creepy noises. The woods weren't silent at all, they were full of life, and not all of it sounded friendly to Jayden.

"Hoot! Hoot!" The noise came so suddenly that it startled Jayden. He jumped off the path and caught his foot in the roots of a tree. He fell over, rolled onto his back and stopped at the base of a tree looking up into its branches.

Two large yellow eyes were watching him. Jayden held his breath and stared into the eyes. They seemed to get bigger and change colour from yellow to pale blue.

"You're as noisy as a herd of cows," came a voice booming from the darkness behind the owl.

Jayden scrambled up onto his feet and looked around in alarm.

"Up here boy!" came the voice again.

Jayden slowly lifted his gaze. The eyes had moved, and were now looking down at him from a branch just above his head. It was an owl; a large one too. The snow-white feathers on its chest and around its eyes glowed in the darkness, and he could make out its faint outline.

"Did you just speak to me?" asked Jayden with a tremor in his voice.

"Of course, I spoke to you! Are there any other clumsy humans about?"

I was just about to head off for a pre-dawn hunt, but if you scare off all the small critters, I'll never get anything decent to eat."

"I'm, I'm sorry, Mr Owl. I've come to the woods to look for the magic mushroom. My Grandpa told me I could find it near the old oak in the heart of the woods."

"Hoot!" The owl fluttered its wings and poised itself on to a low branch right next to Jayden. Jayden could now clearly see the owl. It had a heart-shaped face and the feathers on its back were tawny, marked with white and dark spots, and its beak was squashed down on its face as if someone had punched it in the nose. The eyes kept changing colour from yellow to pale blue.

"You'll never get there if you walk at that pace. The Lion's Mane only shows itself just before dawn, and you don't have a minute to spare if you want to get to it before it shrivels and disappears again."

Strange, Jayden thought, he hadn't mentioned the name of the mushroom to the owl.

"Come on. I'll take you to the old oak before it's too late. The sooner you get out of the woods, the sooner I can get my breakfast. With you roaming about the woods, none of the more interesting animals will come out."

At that moment, Jayden realised that he shouldn't have been afraid of the animals in the woods. They were probably terrified of him. He was traipsing through the woods, thinking he as quiet as a mouse when he sounded more like an elephant to the animals.

His fear suddenly vanished. The owl had given him hope together with wisdom. Maybe there was still a chance to find the mushroom.

So, Jayden followed the owl as it silently spread its wings and flew ahead, like a glowing beacon of silvery feathers. From time to time, the owl would sweep back and fly over Jayden's head. The first time Jayden flinched and covered his head with his arms, but he then found that the owl's presence was reassuring. As they progressed deeper into the woods, the scent of the fir trees gave way to a damper and muggier smell. Young oak trees appeared along the path and got larger and larger with every step Jayden took.

It seemed to Jayden that only five minutes had passed when the owl finally fluttered to a stop perching on the lowest branch of an enormous and majestic oak.

The scent of the ferns filled Jayden's nostrils, and soft decaying leaves carpeted the ground all around him. Pale shreds of light filtered through the thick canopy of the oaks. Dawn was approaching.

The owl cocked its head to one side as if trying to point to something and its eyes glowed a strange pale blue.

"Hurry boy, before it disappears," its voice more impatient than worried.

Jayden crouched down at the base of oak in the direction the owl had nodded. He scrutinised the foot of the oak and walked around its perimeter in vain.

"I can't see anything," whispered Jayden to the owl.

"Patience," said the owl, "remember what I said. Look on the side facing east."

Jayden couldn't remember the owl saying anything about the east. He scratched his head puzzled. It was weird enough that the owl could talk, but Jayden had a familiar tingle in his tummy when the owl spoke, but he couldn't quite figure out what it was.

Grandpa had told Jayden that moss mostly grew on the north side of tree trunks. So, touching the spongy growth with his fingers, he traced an imaginary line to the right of the tree trunk then knelt on the soft ground and riveted his eyes to the base of the tree. He peered hard trying not to blink. A few moments went by then he heard the owl flutter its wings above him. That was when he saw it; nestled between a crack in the bark. The mushroom seemed to grow as Jayden watched. It spread its spongy white tentacles out to catch the faintest yellow glow of dawn barely seeping through the leaves. It reminded Jayden of a soft cluster of coral with dangling tassels, and was as white as the owl's face, glistening with life.

Gingerly, Jayden reached out half expecting it to entwine its feelers around his hand and yank it off. But the Lion's Mane was soft and slightly slimy, making it hard for him to grasp it properly. Using a small penknife, which he always carried with him, Jayden carefully cut through the base of the mushroom, until he had detached it from the tree. He then carefully placed the Lion's Mane in the canvas bag Grandpa had given him.

Jayden looked up in the branches to thank the owl. But the feathered friend had disappeared.

Jayden spun around, suddenly afraid of being alone. But by now, he could clearly see the path along which he and the owl had come. Darkness was giving way to light and Grandpa would soon get better again.

Grandpa had been right. The animals of the woods were their friends.

But was the owl really just an animal or was it something or someone else?

The Miracle of the North

Amy was very excited. In fact, she was over the moon. Her father had promised he would take her to see the magnificent spectacle of the North. Finally, here she was in the Laplands. They had travelled up to the northernmost tip of Sweden by train. It had been a long trip, and Amy had been fretting with excitement all the way. Once they had arrived at their destination, she had had to wait another two days before the great show.

But now, finally, here she was ready for the big night.

After supper, that evening a group of people gathered at the reception of the Ice Hotel where they were staying. Amy listened as the man with a funny looking bright blue woollen hat explained to the guests what the 'aurora borealis' was.

Amy knew this was the official name for the northern lights. She also knew that the bright lights were visible because electrically charged particles from the Sun collided with the Earth's atmosphere. But Amy listened to the man anyway. She knew everything there was to know about the northern lights.

"The auroras are created by solar winds that flow from the Sun past the Earth. These solar winds are charged with particles of ionised gas, which get drawn into our atmosphere and are pulled into the Earth's magnetic field. What happens is that as soon as they enter the atmosphere, these ion particles collide with atoms high up in the air, just like tiny marbles and release an amazing amount of energy. This energy is converted into the fantastic spectacle we can admire from this very point of the Earth. A sight that will leave you in awe," he ended dramatically.

Amy held her father's hand as they followed the group out of the hotel. She glanced at the large clock over the reception area. There were six different clocks, all showing different times in the capitals of the world. The time was now 8.30 p.m. The man had told them that if they were lucky, they might start seeing the first mysterious lights around nine.

They walked into the clear and icy night. The sky was black, and the stars twinkled merrily as if dancing on the black expanse. To Amy's surprise, there were five

Sami sledges with reindeer at the head of each. The Sami people were the natives of the Laplands. They lived in tents and slept under reindeer fur blankets. The Sami leading their sledges were wearing thick royal blue costumes with yellow and red embroidery along the collar and buttons. They were also wearing fur hats lined with the same bright embroidered lining.

"We're going on a sledge ride?" Amy gasped, squeezing her father's hand.

"Surprise!" replied Papa, picking Amy up and dropping her into one of the sledges. They were not very big and could take only three people, including the Sami leading the sleigh.

As soon as Amy settled comfortably between Papa and Mama, they were pulled forward with a jolt, and the sledge started to slide silently on the snow. The soft pounding of the reindeer's hooves was the only sound disturbing the enchanting winter evening.

They whooshed through the frozen darkness towards the mountain that rose to the north of the Sautusjärvi lake, beyond which the forest lay dark and mysterious.

"We only have a short ride," said Papa, as if to reassure them that the chill of the night would not be too bad. But Amy didn't mind. She would have been happy even without the reindeer skins that covered their knees to protect them from the frosty wind.

"If you look towards the mountain you might..." Papa's words stopped in mid-sentence, and Amy felt his hand grip hers. He was pointing with a shaky gloved hand towards the forest.

Amy's mouth dropped open and icy droplets landed on her tongue and pricked her teeth. She was lost for words and thought she might be dreaming or imagining things.

There, over the forest, the night sky was lit up with a wondrous glow. Swirling, silky lights of green and pale yellow were twisting and twirling above the canopy of fir trees.

Amy thought that was how hundreds of fairies would look like, dancing and sliding on ice, their wands leaving trails of bright green and golden magic sparks behind them.

The sledges slowed down, and a chatter of excited voices broke the magic of the mysterious and silent dancing lights.

"We're very lucky tonight," shouted the guide with the funny blue hat, "and we haven't even reached the best spot yet!"

The Sami sledge leader shook the reins again and headed towards the mountain and the woods as the eerie green glow faded, then grew stronger, like a wave breaking on the seashore then retreating back into the sea.

The group had nearly reached their destination when another larger wave hit the black sky. Rays of green and pink shot up like sunbeams from behind clouds. They started to ripple like thick curtains blown around by a strong gust of wind. They swayed and glowed intensely over the forest and the mountain, getting larger and larger.

Amy thought it looked very spooky, and the silence and intense light intensified the eerie atmosphere. She imagined that the thunder which should have followed these lights was being trapped somewhere in the mountain, stifled, and would explode unexpectedly like a large volcano and shatter the mountain to bits.

Amy gripped onto her father and stared as if hypnotised at the glowing sky. The sledges came to a halt, and everyone got out of their cosy seats, all heads tilted towards the glowing heavens above.

Papa took Amy by the hand, and they too got out. The crowd gathered around the lake across from the forest. Here the show was so breathtaking that everyone seemed frozen in with the surrounding snow and ice.

Now, the sky was lit up with multicoloured figurines, which appeared to be dancing on the lake. The display of coloured lights was reflected off the lake's icy surface and the whole night was ablaze with streaming purples and arcs of greens, blues, yellows, pinks and even flickers of red appeared on the outskirts.

Then, out of the ghostly dancing of lights and clouds that were capturing the small group staring across the lake and up at the spectacle above, came an ever so faint noise. The reindeer's ears pricked up and the Sami turned his head and scrutinised the horizon at the base of the mountain.

The sound was similar to that of a crow croaking, and no one else paid attention except for Amy and the Sami.

The reindeer fidgeted a little. They seemed nervous, and the Sami man calmed them down. Amy glanced to the left towards the small mountain. The sky above was scattered with patches of green and purple clouds. The hues were less intense than the ones over the lake. However, there was no mistaking the silhouette that was blotted against the haze of colour.

A large polar bear stood far off at the base of the mountain. Amy could just make out his nose tilted upwards. Next to the large bear a smaller one stood, he too sniffed the air. Amy's eyes widened and filled with tears as the ice-cold breeze pricked her eyes. She couldn't believe what she was seeing. A polar bear and its cub. Her eyes were full of real tears now, tears of emotion, and she could no longer make out the pale silhouettes. When she wiped her eyes dry, they had disappeared swallowed by the night enveloped by the rays of gleaming streamers above them.

Amy turned her head back to the light display over the lake, her eyes brimming with tears again. Mama was watching her, a puzzled expression flickering in her eyes. They, too, were reflecting the green rays from the sky.

"Are you feeling alright, Amy?" she asked her brow troubled.

"I'm fine, Mama," Amy replied with a smile of pure happiness.

And Amy was fine, she was the happiest little girl in the world that night, and the most fortunate. Not only had she seen the most phenomenal spectacle in her whole life. Amy had seen a real polar bear, there in the wild under the magical northern lights.

The Musical Christmas Tree

This year our Christmas tree looked much smaller. I could feel Grandpa watching as I frowned at the prickly green tree. Papa had settled it next to the dining room window so that you could see the lights when you walked up the driveway. But I was sure no one could. The tree was much too small. My nose started tingling, and I quickly wiped away a tear. I didn't want Grandpa to think I was upset because of the tree. I wasn't really. It was just a bit too small.

When we finished decorating the bristly branches with gold and blue tinsel and sparkling silver baubles, the tree was jam-packed. The silver and white paper angels I had made with Mom last year, lay in the box together with discarded strips of golden tinsel.

The star we usually used for the treetop was too big. When Grandpa tried to place it on the top branch, it bent, and the star fell off. Grandpa and I exchanged glances, and he smiled gingerly. I knew he agreed with me, but he couldn't say he disapproved of Papa's choice.

So I handed him one of the angels and another tear rolled down my cheek. This time I didn't bother wiping it away. The truth was I *was* upset.

Finally, we wrapped the string of coloured lights around the overstuffed fir and Grandpa plugged them in. They didn't work, of course. Papa fretted about trying to fix the problem. I said goodnight, and Grandpa said he would tuck me in that night. I knew he was as upset as I was, but we didn't talk about it. Instead, Grandpa told me a bedtime story. Can you guess what the story was about?

It was Christmas time, and the village men were out with their saws and axes cutting down fir trees for the village square. The trees were grand firs and pines, with branches thick with green needles. Once they had felled fifteen good specimens, they started loading them onto a large cart. They had nearly finished when one of the men laughed out loud and said, "Look at this puny tree. How did *that* get in amongst the ones we cut down?" The other men joined in the fun, and one of them threw the stunted fir aside. "Leave it to rot with the other shrubs," he said with a snicker.

At this point in Grandpa's story, I was starting to feel guilty about my feelings towards our Christmas tree. The men in the story sounded mean and nasty.

So there lay the fir tree, too small to be privileged as a Christmas tree and left to its fate until darkness fell over it like a blanket. That night the first winter snowflakes floated gently from the sky and lay around the abandoned fir tree. The small animals of the wood overjoyed with the soft white flakes came out of their burrows and left their nests. They gathered around the fallen shrub that had been discarded on their favourite clearing. They were so thrilled that they decided to throw a winter party and have some fun before the wood froze over entirely for the winter. The robins chirped, and the blackbirds whistled. The owls hooted, and the rabbits tapped their hind legs in rhythm with the feathered orchestra. They danced and danced around the tree and sang their favourite winter songs.

Suddenly the tree shook and trembled, then slowly it rose and stood upright. Its bristly branches glistened with snow crystals and appeared enormous to the animals of the forest. They watched in awe as the sparkling branches swayed and the fir tree started to hum the same winter melody the animals had been singing.

"It's a real Christmas tree," cried out a grey rabbit with a stubby white tail.

"So it is, " said the wise old owl as he flew over the top to examine it more closely.

"It's the most beautiful Christmas tree I've ever seen," added a young doe staring at the singing Christmas tree with its large brown eyes brimming with tears of joy.

All night long the animals of the forest danced and sang around the musical Christmas tree until it was entirely covered in snow.

One by one, the animals fell asleep under the shelter of the little-big tree's branches and dreamt of Christmas lights and goodies, while the fir tree chanted its lullaby until sunrise.

Grandpa tucked me in and kissed my forehead. Without another word, he turned off my bedside lamp and left my bedroom, leaving the door ajar. Strange, I thought, he never does that. Grandpa always closed the door gently after he tucked me in at night.

Then I heard it, a faint trail of notes drifting up from downstairs. It was unlike any sound I had ever heard, like a gentle melody swirling in the snow.

I threw the bedcovers aside and got out of bed. I padded barefoot towards the door and peeked through the gap in the door. Here the music was more intense, and flowing along with it came strange and magical words. They were so enchanting that I felt the urge to follow the invisible trail. They led me through the corridor and down the stairs. The house was dark, but the music now filled the whole house. The golden notes warmed my heart and drew me towards the door that led to the dining room. I turned the handle and slowly pushed the door open.

The little Christmas tree was still there, but it was no longer small and stuffed with oversized decorations. It shone and glittered with snowflake-like lights, and it was singing and playing the most mesmerizing song I had ever heard. I knelt next to it, and as I looked up from my crouched position, the fir tree seemed to rise higher and higher until it stood over me like a giant friend. I sighed and lay down with my head resting on my arm until I fell asleep, cradled by our magical and wonderful Christmas tree.

The Mystery in the Garden

"Come on, Jeremy, run along and tidy your bedroom!"

Here we go again. Every time I try and speak seriously to my parents, up go their eyebrows, and off they send me to do my homework, set the table and of course, tidy my bedroom.

I am not dreaming, I swear I'm not. I saw Bellboom move!

Bellboom is our garden dwarf. He's a funny-looking dwarf, dressed just like any sensible dwarf should; with a red pointed hat, a green jacket and a long white beard. I've always adored Bellboom, and I still remember the time he was actually taller than I was. That, of course, was years ago.

I used to rush out into the garden every morning and stand next to him, to check and see if I'd grown. My father used to watch me in amusement and say with a laugh, "don't worry Jeremy, you'll soon catch up with him!"

Now I'm nine years old, and of course, Bellboom comes up to my belly button, so I have now stopped playing that game with him.

My sister Wendy simply adores him. She hugs and kisses the poor dwarf and dances around him, letting out little screams of joy. Poor Bellboom. He really does have a lot of patience.

This week Bellboom moved a little every day. On Tuesday, I couldn't believe my eyes. He was no longer standing on his usual spot.

"Who moved Bellboom? Was it you?" I asked my dad.

"No, I didn't," replied my father with irritation. "Can't you see I'm busy?"

Indeed, he was, crouched next to the lawnmower, his hands full of grease, trying to puzzle out why it would no longer budge.

On Thursday, he had moved again. This time I went up to my mum, who was busy mixing some strange looking liquid in a bowl, with the telephone stuck between her ear and shoulder.

She just shook her head in annoyance and continued mixing, chattering and splattering the yellow 'stuff' all over the kitchen counter.

This morning I went into the garden, and he had moved right over near the edge of the garden. At this rate, anyone could have stolen him, from right under our noses. I really had to do something and fast.

So, I decided to talk to my grandfather about the problem.

"There is nothing strange about that, Jeremy," my grandfather replied when I asked him what he thought was happening.

"If you had read those books I gave you a little while back more carefully, you would know that some magical creatures just can't stand the daylight. As soon as the first morning rays shine through, they turn into stone."

I knew I could count on Grandpa. I can tell him anything he'll always listen to me.

He lives all alone, a few blocks down from us and on Saturdays, my sister Wendy and I go and visit him.

His answer seemed a bit strange to me, but as I was playing in the orchid patch, I suddenly had a brainwave.

My mother adores gardening, but she never seems to remember to water the plants. This is why; if it doesn't rain or Daddy forgets to get the water hose out from the garage, the ground is as dry as dust.

This was my idea…I would take the hose pipe out of the garage and soak the ground that night, just before bedtime. This would make it nice and muddy, so if Bellboom started wandering about during the night, I would be able to see his footprints and follow his movements.

The next morning I jumped out of bed and ran into the garden in my pyjamas. I couldn't believe my eyes!

There stood Bellboom quietly, surrounded by a multitude of tiny footprints.

I stared at him fixedly, hoping to catch him blinking or shifting a little. But no, he was as still as stone. And I was soon in for more surprises.

At lunchtime, the doorbell rang, and Wendy, my curious little sister, jumped up and ran to open the door. It's incredible how nosy she is!

We were all in for a surprise. It was Grandpa. He never goes anywhere since our grandma died, and I wondered if everything was alright.

"You're looking great, Grandpa, "my mother said. "Please stay and have lunch with us all."

"With great pleasure," replied my grandpa, smiling knowingly towards me.

With that, Wendy took his hand gleefully and pulled him to the dining table and stubbornly demanded to sit on his knee throughout the whole of lunchtime.

After lunch, Grandpa took me to one side and asked me if I had solved the mystery.

I led him to the garden and showed him the footprints in the mud.

Grandpa examined the footprints and then looked at me with a puzzled expression.

"There is something I just can't figure out," he mumbled. "Think a bit, Jeremy. What colour are your sister's eyes?"

"Well, brown I think," I answered.

"You're not sure? She's your sister, after all. Ponder over this for a while, then let me know."

Grandpa left me there in the mud, deep in thought.

" What an odd question to ask," I thought to myself. "What's that got to do with Bellboom?"

Still intrigued, I decided to clear this doubt and went off to look for Wendy.

I was baffled to find that her eyes were actually blue. I could have sworn they were brown like mine.

Grandpa stayed with us all day and just before saying good-bye he slipped a piece of paper into my hand.

"There are two questions to your mystery. First of all, how can Bellboom's footprints leave shoe prints, when he doesn't have any shoes in the first place? Secondly, don't you think a brother really should know what colour his sister's eyes are?"

I thought about this puzzle all through the night, and I still couldn't figure out what my sister had to do with the mystery.

Suddenly all was clear! I rushed into my sister's bedroom, and she wasn't there.

At the foot of her bed lay a pair of muddy slippers. There was no longer any doubt.

I silently climbed down the stairs and go out into the garden. There was Wendy deep in conversation with Bellboom.

"Come, Bellboom, you'll be better off here," she said, lifting the garden dwarf with great effort and moving him to the left. "You'll be able to see the birds' nests from here."

She chatted and sang to him and even told him stories. Now I understood what Grandpa was trying to say to me. My grandpa was right.

Wendy tells Bellboom all those secrets she can't tell me because I never listen, and he listens more than I ever do. I can't even remember the colour of my sister's eyes.

Then, I call out to my sister in a whisper. She glances up at me and smiles radiantly, runs up to me and gives me a whacking kiss on my cheek.

"Why don't you jump up onto my back?" I ask with a smile. "You'll be able to see the birds' nests better from up here."

We laugh as we run around the house at least ten times, and we've never had so much fun before tonight.

Since then, Bellboom has never moved again. Sometimes when I look at him closely, I can catch him winking at me from the end of the garden.

The Seashell Boy

Akela lifted a small ivory-coloured shell streaked with wisps of brown and orange. She peered into the oval opening to make sure its inhabitant had left home for good. It wouldn't be fair to take the shell if the crab was still living in it. She dropped it into the small yellow bucket poised on the rock beside the pool she was exploring. Her gaze returned to the shallow pool of seawater, and she crouched down to examine the hidden life. Minute semi-transparent shrimps were darting in every direction.

Akela smiled at the hectic dance. She loved exploring the rock pools by herself, especially today. The ocean breeze carried the pungent smell of seaweed and the distant waves breaking on the coral reef, soothed Akela's distress. No one cared about her anymore. Her mother was always talking about the new baby, and her father kept buying fresh mangoes to keep Mother happy and the baby healthy. Nobody thought of buying chocolate ice cream for Akela to keep *her* happy.

The yellow bucket wobbled and tipped. Akela caught it by the handle just in time and settled it between her pecan brown knees.

Frowning, she peered inside. Nothing was stirring in the bucket. She watched to see if a crab was trying to get out of the shell she had just picked. But nothing stirred. Her dark brow creased and she looked more closely at the shell. She was sure it hadn't been that big when she had picked it from the pool. She rubbed her eyes then blinked three times as the salt from her hands stung her large brown eyes.

It was time to get back for tea before her mother got cross because she was late. Mother was often irritable now. She hardly ever read Akela bedtime stories. Mother went to bed early nowadays. Father said she needed extra rest for the baby. So Akela had to read her on her own. Father said she was older now, and she should practice reading on her own. Of course, Akela was a good reader, but she missed Mothers warm voice as she narrated of faraway lands, lulling her to sleep.

Akela took the bucket filled with seawater and decided not to empty it just in case there *was* a crab in the shell. In that case, she would take it back to the pool and keep only the empty shells.

Mother didn't get angry with Akela for arriving late, she was resting on the bed while Father prepared the tea.

"Mother needs to nap for the baby," explained Father with a lame smile when he offered Akela a plate with a runny egg and a lump of rice on the side. Akela hated runny eggs, and she hated the baby even more.

That night when Father came to kiss her good night, he didn't volunteer to read a bedtime story. He said he had to go and check if Mother and the baby were alright. Akela turned off her bedside light and lay in her bed, alone and heavyhearted. She eventually fell asleep with tear-streaked cheeks and dreamt of the rock pools and the rumble of the waves.

The crashing of the waves got louder and louder until the noise shook Akela awake. She gasped and held on to the sides of her bed. Her breathing came in rapid breaths, and she inhaled deeply as she came out from the troubled dream. She was about to get out of bed and run to her parents' bedroom, but she stopped. Father would probably get cross because Akela had disturbed

Mother. So, Akela turned on her side to switch on the bedside light. The yellow bucket she had left beside her bed and fallen over, and there was a large puddle of water all over the bamboo floorboards.

Oh dear, thought Akela I'll get into trouble if I don't clear up this mess. So she got out of bed tiptoeing in the water and picked the bucket up. Most of the shells were still in the bottom, so she picked up the few that were lying in the puddle and returned them to the bucket. That was when she noticed that the last shell she had found, the one with the lovely streaks was missing.

Akela frowned, took a beach towel from the back of a chair, and started mopping up the water. As she knelt in the pool trying to soak up the mess, an entrancing melody drifted from somewhere under the bed. Her dark eyebrows knitted and warily she lifted the bed covers that had draped to the floor and peered under the bed.

Akela's eyes widened with amazement, and she let out a cry. The missing shell was lying under her bed, quaking as soft notes that reminded Akela of the sounds of the ocean floated out from the ivory casing. But it wasn't the music that surprised Akela.

The seashell was now the size of a large tortoise and trembled vigorously with the music. Akela was terrified that a gigantic crab would crawl out and pinch her hard with its claws.

The tune faded and stopped, and the most amazing thing happened. The seashell toppled over and there next to it, sitting cross-legged, sat a miniature boy staring at her with intense dark blue eyes.

"Who are you? stammered Akela.

"I'm the boy with no name, and I've come so you can tell me what it is."

"How am I supposed to know what your name is?" asked Akela even more confused.

"Well, I was hoping you could as you're my sister."

He lowered his long dark lashes, and a tiny tear rolled down his pale cheek. His skin was the colour of the ivory shell, and his hair was black speckled with silver like the granite rocks of the ocean.

Akela's emotions were a mix of astonishment and sadness. How could this boy possibly be her brother? And why was he so sad? Akela imagined that she would also be sad if she didn't have a name. She squeezed her eyes shut. *This must be a dream, and when I open my eyes, the tiny creature will have disappeared.*

But then she heard the faint voice again. "I know you hate me, though I don't understand why. I hear your voice every day, and I'm already fond of you."

Akela shook her head and opened her eyes. "What do you mean, you hear my voice every day. You were living in that shell a few hours ago, and I fished you out from a rock pool."

"I wasn't living there before, a crab was. I just borrowed the shell so I could come to ask you about my name."

Akela's head was whirling faster. "So where do you come from?"

"From our mother's womb, of course."

Akela gasped and hit her head on the underside of the bed frame.

"I'm the baby you hate so much."

"How's that possible," stammered Akela, "you can't just come out of Mother and pass through a seashell.

"I can if I'm very, very unhappy. How can I come into this world if my sister doesn't want me and she won't even call me by name?"

The miniature boy lowered his eyelashes and sighed deeply. He looked so fragile and wretched that Akela reached out for him and picked him up with both hands, together with the shell and placed him delicately on the bed covers. She could see him clearly now. He was beautiful in the light of the bedside lamp. His cheeks as soft as melted butter and his eyes were the darkest and gleaming blue she had ever seen. She felt a deep sadness and guilt. How could she have hated this being if he was indeed her brother?

"I didn't even know you were a boy. Nobody told me."

"That's because our mother doesn't want to know. But I want you to know Akela, I've come all this way from the ocean to the seashell to tell you that I love you very much. Maybe just maybe, if we find a name for me, you might start loving me just a tiny bit."

Another tear rolled down the delicate cheek as the dark blue eyes searched Akela's. She stretched out her hand, and the seashell boy laid his small one in the palm of her hand. It tickled Akela like a feather and carried the warmth of a sunray, spreading to her arm and heart.

"Careful, I'm very fragile and I can't stay with you for long. I have to go back through the seashell to our mother's womb."

At that instant, Akela knew that she had been utterly wrong. She wasn't going to lose on love when the baby arrived, she would be loved even more. Sheer happiness flooded her whole body, and she finally realised how unique she was. Akela was the only one of the family to know that the baby was a boy, and he had come to her to ask her to love him in return. All of a sudden, she was no longer angry with Mother and Father, she couldn't wait to hold her baby brother in her arms and cover him with kisses.

"I'll call you Kai, like the ocean," croaked Akela, overwhelmed with emotions.

Kai smiled, and his delicate face glowed in a haze like the ocean mist.

"Kai," he whispered in a singsong voice, "Kai will see you soon, Akela."

With those last words, he gave Akela a final glance filled with hope and happiness, and he lowered the seashell over him.

Soft music began to drift from the shell again. Akela lay down beside the ivory object and hummed with the magical notes until her eyelids drooped and she fell into a land of dreams. Here the ocean waves gently washed over her as she lay on the heated sand diffusing warmth and happiness.

Uncle Alan's Animal Garden

My uncle Alan has a very peculiar hobby. He collects animals. Not any common animal but all sorts of specimens; domestic, wild, furry, scaly, slithery. They're all enclosed in his large garden and backyard not far from where we live.

Fortunately, they aren't real and won't pounce on you when you cross the garden to get to the house. If you look at them from the garden gate, you would half expect them to start roaring or mooing or even charge at you as you push it open. Most times, I hesitate before entering the overcrowded enclosure. And by the way, these are not just statues. They look so real and some outright menacing.

Your next question might be. Why would someone want to collect such a large number of animals? For fun of course. My uncle is an eccentric and whimsical man. He says he treasures the moment he steps into his fantasy safari land every evening when he gets back home from work. He says it's like travelling the world without leaving your own garden, and that's true in a way.

"There is nothing more restful, Noah my boy, than pushing open the garden gate and entering into my own animal kingdom," he often says.

I know I shouldn't worry about these animals because they're only representations, although they look pretty real. However, there is one puzzling matter I've been thinking more and more about lately.

I'm not sure if I'm imagining this, but the animals seem to change places every time I go and visit.

The other day I casually asked my uncle if he had moved some of them around. He simply replied enigmatically. "Oh, the animals do as they wish, it's their home."

Now, what kind of answer was that? I was sure he was fooling about with me until the weekend came.

My parents were taking my elder brother up north to a snazzy school he had been accepted at for his sixth form year. Everyone was brimming with excitement, except for me. For one, I didn't want my brother to leave home, and two now my mother would give me all the blame for leaving the bathroom untidy and for breaking the glasses.

"You'll be good company for your uncle," said my father as they dropped me off before heading north. I had never thought about my uncle feeling lonely, but I suppose he must have, living all by himself in his big house.

So I got to stay with Uncle Alan, who set my bed up in one of the larger bedrooms where I had a great view of the garden and its residents.

We spent the whole of the Saturday afternoon working in my uncle's vegetable garden. He had loads of carrots and leafy vegetables, as well as strawberries, blackberries and raspberries, and the garden seemed a bit oversized for a man living by himself. I suppose he gave most of his vegetables to the neighbours, or just enjoyed working in the garden. The funny thing was that my uncle worked as a gardener all day long. I couldn't imagine why he would want to work in the garden at the weekends as well.

"Well, someone's got to feed the family," he replied when I asked him later that afternoon.

So, that was where Mum got all her vegetables then, from Uncle Alan, I mused.

For supper, Uncle Alan prepared a delicious leek soup with herbs we had picked from the garden. The whole kitchen was flooded with delicious smells of garlic, parsley and leek, as well as other aromas. Not only was Uncle Alan, a good gardener, he was also a fantastic cook.

"This soup has secret ingredients," replied Uncle Alan when I asked what it was he had added to the leek, "you'll have the most wondrous dreams with a belly full of Alan's secret soup!"

I shrugged, not wanting to show Uncle Alan that I was fazed he wouldn't confide in me, but I was feeling rather sleepy after the hard work in the garden, so I didn't press him for the recipe.

It took some effort to climb the stairs and get into bed. I must have fallen asleep even before Uncle Alan switched off my bedside lamp.

I woke up in the middle of the night, jolted awake by a rattling at the window. I sat up in bed and rubbed my eyes still groggy with sleep. The rattling came again, and I could also hear the faint wail of the wind outside.

It was probably one of the branches of the beech tree next to my window, scratching against the windowpane. I pulled the duvet up close to my chin, and was about to turn over and go back to sleep when I caught a flash of light coming from outside. I sat up and rubbed my eyes harder. The light came again. Curiosity made me find the strength to get out of the warm bed, and I walked barefooted to the window and peered out.

The beam of light was coming from a powerful torch, and it was making its way up the garden path towards the vegetable patch. My first alarming thought was that a thief had gotten into Uncle Alan's garden. I was about to rush to his bedroom and wake him up, but then the beam of light stopped, and it moved to light up the face of the intruder. My Uncle Alan. What was he doing in the garden at this time? Then I noticed a movement right behind him, and Uncle Alan crouched down close to something on the ground.

Suddenly the wind picked up again and swept away the clouds that had been hiding the full moon and my both dropped open. I was sure I was still dreaming, and I probably was. There in the garden, next to my uncle was a baby panda bear, like the statue to the left of the bamboo plant, nibbling on something my uncle had given it.

It was chewing happily. It was moving. It was alive!

But that was no big deal compared to the rest of the display before me. Now that I could see the garden clearly under the silver rays of the moon. I noticed more movement. There was movement everywhere in the garden. Near the pond, where the two turtles and the flamingo usually stood, and in the branches of the eucalyptus tree, where Uncle Alan had perched a mother and a baby Koala. But it wasn't the wind moving the branches and the reeds. The animals were!

All around the garden, the animals that had been as still as stone that afternoon were now moving about or chewing on something. They were having a midnight feast!

I squeezed my eyes shut and counted to ten, then opened them again. But it was worse. Now I could see the baby elephant thud ungracefully up the garden path towards Uncle Alan. It stopped and swung its trunk up in the air, spraying my uncle with water. I chuckled at the scene, and Uncle Alan nearly toppled over with laughter. He then approached the naughty elephant and scratched its head while feeding it with a large bunch of dried leafy vegetables.

The baby elephant backed up and turned around, heading for the trees, its bottom swinging to and fro. The two zebras that were usually to the right of the pond trotted up to my uncle and nuzzled him gently on the shoulder, standing on either side of him. To them too he gave a generous batch of dried leafy vegetables and stroked their striped coat. Suddenly from behind Uncle Alan, the racoon that had been sitting near the gate the last time I had seen it, got up on its hind legs and started pawing at my uncle's sleeve. I could see its cute muzzle twitching and its striped tail trailing under it. Uncle Alan fished out something from a canvas bag and filled the palm of his hands with what looked like the blackberries we had picked that afternoon. The racoon was delighted and picked at the sweet fruit popping the blackberries one by one in its mouth.

I stared in wonderment for what seemed like ages as the animals feasted on my uncle's vegetables and fruits and frolicked around the garden, while others swung in the trees. My uncle watched and occasionally scratched someone's tummy or an ear. Now I realised why he needed all those vegetables, and why he had said that the animals could do as they pleased in their garden.

As my eyelids grew heavy again, I also thought of something else my uncle had said at supper. He had said, "you'll have the most wondrous dreams with a belly full of Alan's secret soup!"

So maybe this was just a dream. I tried to keep my eyes open and watch on as the animals feasted and played, but I was overwhelmed with drowsiness. Before my eyes closed and blotted out this magical animal kingdom, I wondered what ingredients Uncle Alan could have possibly put in his secret leek soup recipe.

The Fireflies that Never Stopped Glowing

"Look! A firefly," whispered Toby to his sister Tina.

"A firefly?" blurted out Tina, flattening her nose against the windowpane of the kitchen window.

They had crept down to the kitchen as soon as they were sure their parents had gone to bed for the night and were now in total darkness pressing their faces against the window.

The night was pitch black outside in the back garden, and the wind was swinging the branches violently, threatening to snap them in two.

"Does that mean there's going to be a storm?" asked Tina, her fair brow scrunched up and her large grey eyes were burning with fear. Tina was terrified of storms.

"Fireflies don't bring on storms silly," said her brother Toby with a chuckle.

"Do they set fire to the garden then? Papa said that there have been a lot of bushfires lately and that we have to be extra careful."

"No, of course not!" replied Toby getting impatient with his younger sister.

"They're just called fireflies because they light up."

Tina frowned in the darkness and pressed her nose harder against the window, cupping her hands on the sides of her eyes.

"They look like they're on fire to me," she said with a tremble in her voice.

"I promise you they're not," said Toby, "I'll show you."

He took Tina by the hand and carefully turned the key in the lock of the door that led to the back garden. A warm gust of wind caught Tina's long, fair hair and whirled it around her face and eyes. For a few seconds, Tina couldn't see anything at all, and she clutched onto Toby's hand.

"There," said Toby triumphantly, "Now, you can see they're only glowing and not on fire."

The wind settled for a moment, and Tina swept her hair away from her face and gasped. Circling all around them were tiny yellowish-green lights. They danced in the night wind, swooping down and toppling over and around as the wind picked up again. They were everywhere, and to Tina, they looked like thousands of tiny light bulbs switching on and off as they sent a secret flashing code.

"They're also known as lightning bugs, but I didn't want to tell you before you saw them and realized they have nothing to do with storms, as you're such a scaredy-cat about storms too," said Toby his white teeth flashing in the dark.

Tina let go of his hand and turned her back to him, turning up her nose towards the glowing bugs rotating around her head.

"Actually, they're not flies at all but sort of flying beetles. We're studying about them in science class, and they are so fascinating!"

And fascinating they were! Tina was dazzled by the gleaming jig as she spun round and round trying to keep track of the glowing bugs, one by one.

"Look," she cried, "there are some on the ground just under the bush over there."

There were indeed a few fireflies scattered under the bushes. These seemed to glow less than those in the air.

"Are those on the ground hurt?" asked Tina, "their glow seems to be fainter, maybe they're dying?" Tina frowned and knelt next to the bush.

Tina was sure that the fireflies were burning to death with all the intense light they were emitting and she said so to Toby.

"What can we do to stop them from destroying themselves?"

Toby raised his eyes to the dark sky and sighed. "They are NOT burning to death Tina. They produce a 'cold light' because of a chemical reaction that happens in their bodies. The light is not at all as hot as a light bulb or a flame would be. Those lying on the ground are female fireflies."

Tina frowned again and pouted. "Are you saying that girl fireflies are not as good at flying as the boys?"

Toby shook his head in desperation and sighed. "It's just a mating ritual. The male fireflies fly around emitting as much beautiful light as they can to attract a female. She just sits there and chooses which bug's light she likes the most."

Tina cupped her chin in her hands as she lay down beside the two fireflies under the bush and stared at them.

"Look," said Toby kneeling beside her. He went close up to the insect with his face then blew gently on it. Immediately it glowed intensely. Tina was fascinated by the mysterious reaction, and she too blew over the bug.

"It's like magic," she exclaimed. And it really was. The two children went around blowing on all the fireflies on the ground giggling and gasping as the insects glowed brightly each time they blew over them. After a while, they got weary, and Tina was feeling a bit sleepy, so she lay down beside the bush and looked up above. The male bugs were still flying around dancing in a whirl and glowing even stronger as gusts of warm air made them spark up at each blow. The two children watched in awe and talked in low voices in the warm summer night, as never before.

Tina was delighted with all the stories Toby knew about lightning bugs, and she wanted to know everything there was to know. She wished she could sleep outside every night and not miss one minute of the fiery dance.

"Unfortunately, fireflies are in danger. All the light pollution we have in the cities destroys their habitat. They need darkness to be able to communicate with each other, so when there's too much light, they can't find each other to reproduce, so they disappear."

A tear trickled from the side of Tina's eye and slipped along her cheek, falling to the grass. "But they can't disappear," she whispered with a knot in her throat, "we must do something to help them!"

"Can't we take them somewhere else to keep them safe?"

Toby turned his head and noticed the tears in his sister's eyes as they caught the glow of the fireflies above. "We can't relocate fireflies; they don't like changing habitat, they wouldn't survive.

Tina nodded. She could imagine how she would feel if they were ever to change houses and move away from her school and friends; she would be devastated.

"Maybe we can put them in a jar and keep them safe in a very dark place so that light pollution can't affect them. We could take them up to the shed and keep them there during the day so that they could get as much darkness as possible!"

Toby smiled at his sister's engagement to defend the cause of the fireflies.

"We could put them in jars and take them to the shed as you say, but we would have to take them back to the garden at night. They need fresh air and the bushes and earth. Would you like to be carried back and forth every night?"

Tina shook her head solemnly in the darkness and followed the flashing dance of green and yellow that continued above her.

"But there *is* one thing we can do," said Toby taking his sister's hand in his.

Tina squeezed it and turned her head to look into her brother's eyes.

"We can make sure we turn off the lights to the back garden every night and creep down after lights and come out here to watch them glow and dance for us all night long."

"Oh, please can we?" whispered Tina as she squeezed Toby's hand even tighter.

"Of course we can," said Toby and put his arm around Tina. "But we must remember to bring our sleeping bags next time!"

They watched the gleaming dots as they lay there in each other's arms until their eyelids closed over the flashing lights. Tirelessly the dazzling party continued throughout the night looking over the sleeping figures until the first rays of sun pierced through the darkness.

The Magic Topaz

"Jacob! I see you're day-dreaming again." Mr.Chandler's coal-black eyes bore into me from over his black-rimmed glasses.

I even detected a snarl as his nostrils flared up and his upper lip curled up towards the tip of his hooked nose.

I shrank behind Betty, who was sitting at the desk in front of me.

"Duck down Jacob, or he'll hurl one of his chalk pieces at you," whispered Betty from behind her English spelling book.

I don't think Mr Chandler likes me. But there you go. I don't like him either. Not only is he impossibly dull, but he is also incredibly nasty.

Some days he can be more annoying than mean, other days like today, he can be nastier than boring. So it really is a no-win situation.

The silence in the classroom made the thudding of his steps sound even louder as he slowly strode towards me.

I quickly flipped my spelling exercise book open and scribbled the date, and on a second quick thought added the number one.

"So, I see you have been listening then, Jacob. Not only have you been listening, but you have listened too hard."

I scratched my head. What was he talking about now?

"Betty, have I started the spelling test yet, did I even remotely mention the number one?"

Betty shook her head vigorously without turning around.

Right. Mr Chandler had obviously only told us to write the date. What was wrong with writing number one now?

"Well, I was getting ready for number one," I mumbled.

"You do not take any initiative in my class. Do you hear boy? Just do what I tell you."

I was holding on tight to my ink pen. So tight, I was afraid the ink would shoot out and blotch the white page with that number one looming up ominously at me. I kept my mouth shut tight, and not because I was scared of Mr Chandler. No, not one bit. I'm scared of my mum. If she sees I've received yet another punishment in class she'll make me clean my sister's bedroom as well as mine.

"Now because you have an advantage over your classmates, you can pop into the stationary room and get me a new box of chalk. I might need an extra piece today." He sneered again as he attempted a smile before walking back to stand behind his desk.

"Go on Jacob, you had better move if you don't want to miss the whole spelling test and only get a chance to listen to the second reading."

I sprang up from my desk and grabbed my chair just in time before it toppled over. I quickly slipped out of the classroom and caught a glimpse of the ashen faces looking up towards our English teacher.

"What a mean man," I hissed under my breath. Why were we so scared of him anyway? All he could do was boss small people around. I liked to imagine his wife nagging at him and making him do all sorts of house duties. A good teacher wouldn't need to boss us around. But I wasn't about to feel sorry for him and his bossy wife. I had to get a move on and get back to the spelling test before I missed too many words.

The stationary room was three doors down the long corridor to the left. Only a faint light fell onto the shiny vinyl floor, as daylight filtered through the frosted panes of the classroom doors. I grabbed the round door knob and turned it to open the door, but the door wouldn't budge.

Today really wasn't my lucky day, I thought in exasperation. I pushed harder, but it wouldn't yield. So I shoved my shoulders against the door and jerked forward as the door suddenly burst open and I was flung into the dark room. I hit something and fell with a thud against one of the shelves. I thought I had escaped the worst, but something hard hit my shoulder and landed with a thud into my open hand. I wrapped my hand round it unconsciously. It felt cold and yet warm in the palm of my hand. I looked into my hand to see what it was, but could hardly make out its shape with only the light from the open door, but it shone warmly against my skin.

I stood up gingerly rubbing the hip I had banged in the fall. I switched on the light to get a better look, and my eyes opened wide at the sight of the object.

"What *is* this?" I spoke out aloud. I was staring at an ancient-looking brooch and set in its middle was a deep blue gem. What was an antique brooch dong in the stationary room? It was no ordinary jewel, not one you would find in one of those jewellery shops in the larger town next to ours. It was more like something you would find in Mr Parsley's antique shop next to the village's bookstore.

I turned it over and ran my fingertips over the shiny surface of the gem. It felt so comforting, yet out of place as it lay there in my hand. It belonged to someone no doubt, but I had a strong urge to possess, and I had to fight and will myself to let go. So I quickly grabbed the first box of chalk I could find and put the brooch on the shelf next to the other chalk boxes. Before I left the room, I took a last peek at the ancient jewel and was again tempted to reach out and touch its brilliant surface. I noticed how intricately cut and beautiful it was. "I wonder how it got there?" I muttered as I switched the light and turned around to back out of the room, closing the door behind me. As I did, I could have sworn the compass glowed in the dark. Strange.

"Despicable!" boomed out Mr Chandler, eyeing me with suspicion as I carefully placed the box of chalk on his desk and quickly took my seat. I started scribbling the word, 'D..e...s...p...' was it an 'I' or an 'A'? I could never quite remember how to spell those 'ible' or 'able' words, but I did have a fifty, fifty chance of getting it right.

I couldn't get past word number five as my thoughts kept trailing to the mysterious compass I had seen in the stationary room. Who could it belong to? I was sure it had glowed when I had left it there on the shelf. I looked out of the window as the words and letters swirled around my head and wondered who had left it there and why it was it had landed on me of all people.

The end of the lesson bell rang, and we all handed our spelling tests as we left the classroom. I tried to avoid Mr Chandler's frown as I gave him mine with only five words out of ten scribbled on the paper.

I had to get back to the stationary room and take another peek at the brooch. It was as if it was pulling me towards it, an irresistible force I couldn't oppose. I sneaked along the corridor, making sure nobody was watching and pushed the stationary door open. This time it didn't get stuck, and I quickly slipped into the dark room again. Sure enough, the brooch was there on the shelf where I had left it. Before I could stop myself, I snatched it up and pocketed the object, and in two seconds, I was out in the corridor, heading towards the stairs.

I was about to reach the top of the stairs when I stopped in my tracks. Mr Chandler was coming out of the classroom with a pile of books in his arm. As he closed the door after him, a book slipped, and all the others followed scattering on the floor right in front of my feet.

I cringed waiting for him to yell at me and tell me it was my fault, but he simply chuckled and said. "What a clumsy man I am! Jacob, would you mind giving me a hand to pick up these books, I have to return them to the library before Miss Lavender comes looking for them. The poor lady has got enough work as it is."

I couldn't believe my ears. Was Mr Chandler talking amiably to *me?* He had never been kind to anyone and certainly not to the librarian who was always lugging books up and down the stairs for Mr Chandler's classes. Never once had he offered to carry any for Miss Lavender. Lost for words I helped him pick up the books and each with a smaller pile in our arms we headed up to the second floor to the library.

As we walked in Miss Lavender's deep blue eyes widened and she too remained speechless. Mr Chandler put down the books gently and smiled warmly at her. "There you go Miss Lavender," he said with a nod, "Jacob and I had the bright idea to bring these books up to you today. That will save you one journey at least."

Not only was Mr Chandler smiling, but he was also being charitable and empathic towards Miss Lavender and me. With that, he turned his heels and went out of the library. We both watched him leave our mouths open in amazement, and I stuck my hands in my pockets, not knowing what to do or say. I was embarrassed by Miss Lavender's gaze. I've always had a soft spot for her, she is so sweet and helpful, and has the most amazing gentle blue eyes I've ever seen. The smooth gem in my pocket was warm and seemed to be throbbing.

"Was that Mr Chandler or was I dreaming?" asked Miss Lavender.

I just looked at her wondrous blue eyes and reflected on how similar her eye colour was to the gem I had in my pocket. It seemed to be pulsating even more now.

"I'm not sure," I replied, stammering a little. "It's the first time Mr Chandler has ever been nice to me, but it must be him, he came out of our class with these books, and then all of a sudden he smiled at me!"

"Yes!" exclaimed Miss Lavender, "and he smiled at me too. That was very thoughtful of him to bring these heavy books back and of you too, of course."

My face went all hot, and the gem in my pocket shuddered and twitched so violently that I jumped and pulled the jewel out and opened the palm of my hand. Miss Lavender stared at the gem and then back at me. It was still glowing and we both watched it dumbfounded.

"Where did you get that?" she asked her blue eyes shining like the gem.

I couldn't lie to her, she was the most generous and kind person I had ever met, and I knew I could trust her.

"It fell on me in the stationary room when I went to fetch some chalk for Mr Chandler, and I couldn't resist it, so I took it. I'm sorry," I said my eyes pleading.

"Do you know what kind of gem it is Jacob?" she asked, her eyes brightening up even more.

I shook my head. All I knew was that it was as deep blue as her eyes.

"Jacob, this is a blue Topaz, and it must surely be a very special one. In fact, it might be the lost Topaz that belonged to the first headmistress of the school. Her name was Miss Violet, and they say that she was the kindest and most compassionate teacher there ever was."

Not like Mr Chandler, I thought. How strange his reaction had been.

"How long ago was that?" I mumbled wondering how it was it had landed on me of all people.

"Oh, years and years ago now. I know all about her because one of the history teachers wrote a book about Miss Violet. Come, Jacob, I'll show you."

I couldn't believe my luck, Miss Lavender was showing me of all people a unique book *and* she wasn't even angry with me for taking the gem.

"See, Jacob this is Miss Violet here," she said as she pulled out a hardcover book and showed me the sleeve inside the book. A white-haired lady was poised with dignity; a warm smile illuminating her face. She wore a grey wool jacket and on the left lapel to my amazement I saw the blue gem. It was exactly the same as the one I was holding.

"But Miss Lavender, I didn't steal it, I swear it just landed on me," I stammered again.

"Of course you didn't Jacob no one is accusing you. There must be a reason you came across it. Did you know that Topaz gems are supposed to promote kindness and compassion as well as empathy? It is said that if you wear a Topaz or if you are anywhere near one, it enhances feelings of joy and empathy."

Suddenly we both stared at each other and were struck by a sudden lightning thought. I opened the palm of my hand again, and the Topaz shone brightly lighting up Miss Lavender's eyes even more.

"Is it possible?" she whispered, "could this be Miss Violet's way of promoting feelings of joy to teachers who have to learn to be kinder and more empathetic?

She founded the school with the motto *Kindness kindles great minds*."

My head reeled. I was feeling so dizzy at the thought that Miss Violet could possibly have chosen me as an ambassador to spread kindness to those in need with this magical Topaz. I felt tiny and frightened. I stretched my hand towards Miss Lavender wanting to give it to her.

"No Jacob, Miss Violet obviously wanted a child to have it. It will be our secret, but you must always keep it in your pocket when you come to school. You're the one who is around Mr Chandler most of the time, and I'm sure he's not making life easy for you and the rest of the class. The more he's around you and the Topaz the kinder he will get. This is what Miss Violet wanted, I'm sure."

I felt overwhelmed. I couldn't believe the gem was magic, but obviously, it had some extraordinary power over people. Even Miss Lavender, who was usually pleasant enough, seemed ever sweeter than ever today.

"You have a mission Jacob," she said her deep blue eyes blazing, "you have to bring back Miss Violet's principles of kindness and empathy. You're the one she chose, and she has given you the key to success."

I nodded and gulped down hard. "If you say so, Miss Lavender."

Her deep blue eyes sparkled and then she winked at me and said. "Call me, Violet!"